Perversion

Also by Robert J. Stoller, M.D.

Sex and Gender: On the Development of
Masculinity and Femininity

Splitting

Sex and Gender Volume II: The Transsexual
Experience

Perversion
The Erotic
Form of Hatred

ROBERT J. STOLLER, M.D.

PANTHEON BOOKS
A Division of Random House, New York

Library of Congress Cataloging in Publication Data

Stoller, Robert J.
  Perversion: The Erotic Form of Hatred.
  Bibliography: pp. 221–231.
  Includes index.
  1. Sexual deviation. 2. Hostility (Psychology)
I. Title.
RC557.S76   616.8′583   75–10363
ISBN 0–394–49777–5

Grateful acknowledgment is made to the following for permission to reprint previously published material:

American Medical Association: For "Pornography and Perversion," by Robert J. Stoller, originally published in *Archives of General Psychiatry* 22(1970), 490–499, Copyright 1970, American Medical Association; and for "Symbiosis Anxiety and the Development of Masculinity," which appeared in *Archives of General Psychiarty* 30(1974), 164–172, Copyright 1974, American Medical Association.

The American Psychiatric Association: For "The Impact of New Advances in Sex Research on Psychoanalytic Theory," by Robert J. Stoller, reprinted from pages 241–251 and 1207–1216 of the *American Journal of Psychiatry*, Vol. 130. Copyright © 1973 by the American Psychiatric Association.

The Institute of the Pennsylvania Hospital: For Robert J. Stoller's article, "The Concept of Perversion," No. 10, 1973, of the *Strecker Monograph Series*, published in Memory of Edward A. Strecker, M.D.

International Journal of Psycho-Analysis: For Robert J. Stoller's article "Hostility and Mystery in Perversion."

The Johns Hopkins University Press: For Robert J. Stoller's article "Does Sexual Perversion Exist?" from *Johns Hopkins Medical Journal*, Vol. 134, pages 43–57, 1974.

Contents

Acknowledgments

I want to thank Nathan Leites, Ph.D., whose concern for clear and precise language again served as a conscience I could only sometimes evade, and my secretary, Thelma Guffan, whose patience and skill continues to ease the effort of writing.

Introduction

Why in this enlightened day would one choose to entitle a work "perversion," a term that is becoming passé? The great research published in the last decade or two has taught us that aberrant sexual behavior is found in other species, is ubiquitous in man, and is the product of brain and hormonal factors that can function independently of anything we might call psyche. Then too, their findings make researchers regret society's moral stance that sexual aberration is unnatural—sinful—and the repressive social action that follows. Thus, in ridding ourselves of the concept of perversion, we have the tempting combination of good research serving a humane cause. Yet it is my contention, explored in the body of this book, that perversion exists.

The connotations of the word are unpleasant and have a flavor of morality and therefore of free will that is antiquated in these days of science and determinism. It is to avoid just such connotations that the softer terms "variant," "deviation," or "aberration" are used. More and more these days, decent people—many of them scientists—are concerned about the price their fellows, and even more, whole societies, pay in the effort to suppress victimless aberrant sexual behavior. And so, in the name of decency, it has become the style, using the trappings of Science, to try to get rid of the concept of perversion. This is done not only by changing the term to ones with less severe implications but by trying to show that there are no (or very few) states that actually fit the nasty connotations of "perversion." These workers reach their conclusions by objective means that they feel avoid the dangers of introspective material, such as by studying brain mechanisms in animal and man, which reveal capacities for aberrant behavior inherited and laid down in hormonal organizations of the central nervous system; by statistics that unmask how widespread are these allegedly heinous acts; by anthropological studies that show aberrant sexual behavior to have been the usual—not the exceptional—throughout history and across cultures; and by observation of or experimentation on intact animals. In all these cases, data have been gathered disclosing that aberrant sexual practices are found throughout animal species and are ubiquitous in human behavior. It is easy, then, to conclude that the widespread aberrance in man does not really signify willed behavior—that is, sinfulness, disobedience to accepted morality—but rather a natural tendency of the sexual impulse in the animal kingdom.

Conversely, others—philosophers and essayists rather than formal researchers—who serve a different but also admirable decency try to call us back from the abyss of licentiousness, pointing up the dehumanized, unloving aspects of sexual behavior that emphasizes anatomical more than interpersonal gratification. To need to reduce another person to a breast or a penis or a bit of cloth before one can succeed in concentrating one's lust is very sad—and dangerous; such severe failure of potency and degradation of lovingness only augment the other processes that today disintegrate one's humanity.

The first group of workers wants to be rid of the concept of perversion because it has moral connotations that have no place in the scientific study of behavior and because the term can be used by the repressive forces in society. The other group wants "perversion" retained because we need a sin-laden word to preserve the old morality, which, tested for so long, gives structure to society.

There is some truth in each posture. But both are wrong.

The purpose behind this book is not to describe and discuss the perversions and not to offer a comprehensive theory of the origins and dynamics of perversion, but rather to find the meaning of "perversion," to define the term clinically so that one can recognize the common factor when it appears, regardless of the specific behaviors that make one perversion different from another. To do this, I shall look primarily at hostility, which I find the defining factor.

First, perversion is the result of an essential interplay between hostility and sexual desire, hostility that is manifest in the connotations of the term. (The dictionary, in dealing with "perverse," "perversion," and "to pervert," uses words like corrupt, wicked, incorrect, improper, stubborn, obstinate, wrongheaded; to misdirect, make use of willfully in a wrong or improper manner, misuse, misinterpret, misconstrue, misapply, debase [Webster, 1961].) Second, people with perversions feel (are made to feel) an unending sense of being dirty, sinful, secretive, abnormal, and a threat to those finer, unperverse citizens who are supposed to make up the majority of society. Third, the word itself reflects the need of individuals in society to keep from recognizing their own perverse tendencies by providing scapegoats who liberate the rest of us in that they serve as the objects of our own unacceptable and projected perverse tendencies. All that unsavory sense of sin is lost in the blandness of a term like "variant," with its conspicuous yearning for respectability and statistical cleanliness. (While I can stomach the term "perversion," however, the vicious im-

plications of calling someone a "pervert" make me almost unable to use that word.)

This book is the fourth in a series on the subject of
the development of masculinity and femininity. When
that work began in 1958, I did not expect it to lead to
a study on the meaning of sexual aberrations. But I
have recently found myself believing that perversion
arises as a way of coping with threats to one's gender
identity, that is, one's sense of masculinity and
femininity, for that is the case in the patients I treat.
Now and in coming years the task is to see if the hypothesis that perversions are usually disorders of masculinity and femininity is generally true and not just a
coincidental finding in the few patients I have studied.
In these introductory remarks, I also wish to underline
that thinking in terms of masculinity and femininity
gives a different (though not contradictory) perspective
from that of classical psychoanalytic metapsychology
with its neuter coloration—ego, id, superego, neutrali-
zation, cathexis, and so forth.

A few words about my writing style are in order here
at the start. The reader will soon see that although the
hypotheses are drawn from clinical material, the general-
izations are often stated as if they were not still to be
proved and as if I had studied enough cases to permit
positive statements. But if, as you read, you bear in mind
that these ideas are tentative, we can be spared the excessive use of "it seems" and "perhaps." Treat the book as
an argument to be considered, worked against, and
tested.

In addition, because I do not believe that the technical
language of psychoanalysis is usually necessary, the
reader may miss the weightier quality present in analytic
discussions of sexuality. I do not believe, however, that
an author has said anything more when he habitually
uses words like "cathexis," "narcissism," or "neutraliza-
tion." Important psychological issues can usually be ac-

curately expressed in ordinary language, with the added advantage that any weakness in the argument or data is more visible to both author and reader when the tone is informal.

Because I believe this, I also believe psychoanalysts, when dealing with clinical matters, should write—at the same time—for analysts *and* for others. (Freud is the model.) It forces one to be clearer. Problems in analytic theory that we cannot make most competent and motivated people understand probably cannot be made clear to our fellow analysts either. (The disadvantage herein is that at times I have had to review for the nonanalyst subjects every analyst knows well and have also in a few places referred to work of analysts that will be unfamiliar to some nonanalysts. I have tried to keep those paragraphs few and short.)

Another reason for writing about perversion rather than *the* perversions is my belief that to attempt the latter would be premature. Although there are compendia of bizarre cases, the emphasis in these works has been on superficial case reports with a buckshot spray of etiological theories, veneered with pseudoscience. The theoretical discussions give too many glib answers, and even the case material, at first glance so detailed, is superficial, incomplete, inaccurate. Keeping that in mind, I shall not take up all the aberrations but shall consider a specific condition in detail only to illustrate hypotheses.

I hope, then, that this book will induce readers to check if in truth there is not this lack of information, in the hope that some of those who recognize it will be encouraged toward further study. For there appears to be an odd situation regarding research in aberrant sexual behavior: the relative absence of discussion in recent years gives the impression that not much is left to be done. Extended case material is rarely published in the psychiatric or psychoanalytic literature, as if the cri-

teria for diagnoses were clear-cut, the nature of the
syndromes so evident that detailed descriptions were
quaint, no longer necessary. (Perhaps too many profes-
sionals feel that the studies early in the century by such
workers as Krafft-Ebing and Havelock Ellis have given
us a surfeit of description.) The analytic literature
rarely reports on syndromes other than homosexuality
and fetishism. The two or three papers that appear
each year too often (though with a few wonderful exceptions) just rework a prior theoretical position.
Would it not be better to publicize our ignorance so
that we can move ahead in our understanding of sexual
behavior?

We have a start at remedying this if we separate out
those sexual aberrations produced primarily as a lifelong
attempt to "cure" certain psychic stress from those in
which that dynamic is not at the root of the behavior; I
believe that perversion, but not all aberration, is a product of anxiety and that perverse sexual behavior has
sprinkled through it remnants, ruins, and other indicators of the past history of one's libidinal development,
especially in the dynamics of one's family. If the observer
knew *everything* that had happened in the life of the person he is studying, he would find these historical events
represented in the details of the manifest sexual act. The
observer would then know when and why this person
gave up what he would have most liked erotically, to
choose the alternatives that are the perversion's scenario. This hypothesis, then, is that the perversion is a
fantasy put into action—a defensive structure raised
gradually over the years in order to preserve erotic pleasure. The desire to preserve that gratification comes
from two main sources: (1) extreme physical pleasure
which by its very nature demands repetition; (2) a need
to maintain identity.

I do not see how fantasy can be left out of one's calcu-
lations about human sexual behavior; it is no secret that

fantasy, in the form of daydreams, is present consciously
in much of sexual activity. In fact, on hearing of a person
without sexual fantasy, we suspect that an inhibition is in
force. But run through the names of the great researchers on sexuality of the past generation or more. You will
note that no matter what area they study, or what techniques they use, or what findings they report, they have
produced data of sexual aberrance not motivated by fantasy, that is, not motivated by storytelling that fashions
a new, better "reality." These workers emphasize the
noninvented, nonconflictual, extrapsychic origins of sexual excitement, whether perverse or not. They treat intrapsychic manifestations as if not there. Example: a
handful of cases have been found in the whole immense
universe of man in which aberrant sexual behavior was
set off by a CNS seizure; conclusion: perversion is the
result of epilepsy. Example: free-ranging animals occasionally use a component of the reproductive behavior of
the opposite sex, as when a cow mounts another cow
momentarily; conclusion: homosexuality is part of animal activity, and man, being part of the animal world, is
only expressing his natural inheritance when he is homosexual. Example: a male chimpanzee in New Orleans
masturbates while fondling a boot; conclusion: fetishism
is the result of simple conditioning. Example: certain
societies consider as nonperverse, sexual activity we
define as perverse; conclusion: the act, performed in our
society with the same anatomy, has the same meaning to
the individual and springs from the same psychic sources
as in the alien culture.

And on and on. Such studies unite in an effort to
disprove psychic motivation by substituting primeval
forces like evolution, chromosomal and genetic inheritance, neurophysiology, and conditioning and imprinting that act on a defenseless psychobiology, or by
proclaiming that normative is normal. I disagree, but I
do believe these factors are (or in some cases yet un-

proved, may be) essential inputs to human sexuality. I ask only that we also reckon with the intrapsychic effects of a person's past, especially as expressed in the subtleties of interpersonal relationships. Those who consider themselves scientists may be making a historic mistake in avoiding this factor. They do not know that what is labeled one's behavior is actually also one's explanations. Its complexity at present puts the mind beyond the grasp of experimental techniques; research methods of the scientific establishment are not yet competent to reveal or probe fantasy. But if fantasy exists, it can be studied. And while we wait for science to catch up, perhaps we should turn to that uncertain and yet powerful technique of discovery, the psychoanalytic method, and its bemused offspring, analytic theory.

The goal of my research is to find psychological origins for what I have labeled "gender identity," that is, masculinity and femininity. For doing so, there seem to be three methods in which analysts are most skilled. (1) Analyze adults and children to glimpse roots of their behavior. For generations this has been the source of analysts' insights; the perspective is primarily intrapsychic (ego, superego, id; conscious, preconscious, unconscious; fixation and regression; defense mechanisms; fantasy; and the like). Let us hope, however, that Freud's analogy of the analyst searching the past like an archaeologist does not encourage anyone to be satisfied that a psychoanalysis tells us all we need to know of the past. If you had a chance and you were a historian, would you prefer to pick over the ruins or visit the living city? So we should also (2) observe mothers with their children, plus fathers, plus the family interacting; such studies in the past generation have tested and expanded the findings from (1). (3) Analyze the parents, especially mothers, of the people whose behavior is the object of our research; in the past dozen years, after some years with only the first two, I have concentrated on this last method for the insight it gives into the pressures brought to bear on the child who is to become aberrant. (My colleagues treat the child and one of the parents while I analyze the other parent.)

Working this third way, however, does not indicate a belief that sexual aberrations can be adequately understood by such study; my work is at best complementary to the main body of psychoanalytic findings. We need to draw on data gathered from all three methods.

Perversion, then, is the result of family dynamics that, by inducing fear, force the child who yearns for full immersion in the oedipal situation (desire to possess the parent of the opposite sex and identify with the parent of the same sex) to avoid it. Heterosexuality is a complicated state in that it takes frustration and pain to produce it, and yet (different) frustration and pain also reduce it. If we are to understand this in the individuals we study, we must learn the precise nature of the frustrations and pains to help us see why the different outcomes result. One will understand the origins of perversion best if one views it as blighted heterosexuality; as we shall see, that is not true for all aberrations.

Of course, now I am in the soup, for, like other analysts, I also believe that most sexual behavior, not just that labeled perverse, is the result of life experiences, of conflicts survived and compromises imposed, so that if we look closely enough with our microscope, the idea of normality (other than normativeness) crumbles. We must, for instance, face the ubiquity of sexual pathology in heterosexuals, who are the alleged normals used when we set out to designate abnormals. Until we understand heterosexuality instead of taking it for granted as a given, we will not understand perversion. And to lessen this state of ignorance, we must begin by recalling that heterosexuality is an acquisition; we cannot brush the issue aside by saying that heterosexuality is preordained, necessary for the survival of the species and therefore biologically guaranteed. We have no right simply to accept this unproved, though sensible, biological postulate as being as true in humans as in bees or rats.

On the other hand, there are a number of aberrations that do not originate as compromises forced on one by anxiety. As I use the terms, not all aberrant sexual acts are perversions.

We need definitions now.

Part I

Definition

Chapter 1

Definitions

Let me say what I think an aberration, a variant, and a perversion are and in later chapters review data and concepts that led to the definitions. I believe that perversion does exist; that its harsh connotations reflect a dim awareness that at the core of the perverse act is desire to harm others; and that the concept should be retained, not because it is a useful propaganda weapon for preserving society, but because the condition is demonstrable.

By *aberration* here I mean an erotic technique or constellation of techniques that one uses as his complete sexual act and that differs from his culture's traditional, avowed definition of normality. Sexual aberrations can be divided into two classes: variants (deviations) and perversions.

By *variant* I mean an aberration that is not primarily the staging of forbidden fantasies, especially fantasies of harming others. Examples would be behavior set off only by abnormal brain activity, as with a tumor, experimental drug, or electrical impulse from an implanted electrode; or an aberrant act one is driven to *faute de mieux;* or sexual experiments one does from curiosity and finds not exciting enough to repeat.

Perversion, the erotic form of hatred, is a fantasy, usually acted out but occasionally restricted to a daydream (either self-produced or packaged by others, that is, pornography). It is a habitual, preferred aberration necessary for one's full satisfaction, primarily motivated by hostility. By "hostility" I mean a state in which one wishes to harm an object; that differentiates it from "aggression," which often implies only forcefulness. The hostility in perversion takes form in a fantasy of revenge hidden in the actions that make up the perversion and serves to convert childhood trauma to adult triumph. To create the greatest excitement, the perversion must also portray itself as an act of risk-taking.

While these definitions remove former incongruities, they impose on us the new burden of learning from a person what motivates him. But we are freed from a process of designation that did not take the subject's personality and motivation into account. We no longer need to define a perversion according to the anatomy used, the object chosen, the society's stated morality, or the number of people who do it. All we need know is what it means to the person doing it; while this may be difficult for us to uncover, there is still no a priori reason to reject this technique for defining.

Analysts (and others) have used terms like "aberration," "deviation," or "perversion" as synonyms and classified an act as such according to the observer's, not necessarily the participant's, criteria. Then, when a theory of perversion has been established—preoedipal and oedipal conflict; oral, anal, or phallic fixation and regression; fantasies of threatening objects, such as father's bad introjected penis or mother's worse breast; splitting of the ego; attack or permission by a flawed superego; or whatever—the explanation is complete before one ever sees the patient. To avoid such efficiency, I am trying to force us back for information upon the actual person doing the act. By now it is notorious that the foregoing systems have been offered as explanations for every sort of behavior, which of course means they explain little; with all their strength in describing dynamics, these concepts cannot answer how perversion differs from, say, a tic, a hallucination, mania, or a craving for pickles.

For instance, it is suggested that the perverse act provides gratification because, among other listed "specific indicators of perversion,"

> through it [the act] he [the prototypical patient] acted out a confrontation of idealized and degraded images of his mother . . . it gratified sadistic and masochistic wishes that were otherwise unacceptable . . . castration anxiety and guilt—which he would ordinarily experience in the sexual relation—were successfully warded off by the perverse defensive system . . . the perversion acted out a forbidden wish in disguised form—specifically, both the oedipal wish and the homosexual transference . . . it reenacted the primal scene . . . it also reenacted childhood seduction and gratification by the parents . . . it permitted actual gratification by an actual substitute object, so that the anxiety of object loss was allayed. . . . (114, p. 47)*

We may be allowed a sense of *déjà vu.*

Within the usual psychoanalytic framework we assume that all sexual aberrations are energized by pathological dynamics and treat our patients—and create theory—accordingly. Then, because we use these psychoanalytic concepts to imply disturbance, we find ourselves using that paragon, "the heterosexual," or, even vaguer, "the normal," as the base line for measuring the pathology of those less blessed. Having done that, however, we are driven to the deceit of ignoring our knowledge of the ubiquitous malfunctioning of "the heterosexual" or our failure to find or describe "the normal."

*Full citations of publications quoted or referred to in this book may be found in the list of References on pages 221–231. Numbers in parentheses refer to numbered items on this list.

I prefer definitions anchored in clinical data rather than in theory, and so shall now set out several suggestions and hypotheses, based on observation, that will help elaborate these definitions.

First, when we use the word "sexual" in "sexual aberrations," we should restrict it to conscious erotic excitement and avoid the larger psychoanalytic meanings, which call all pleasure "sexual"; this latter use has value in certain contexts but would only muddle us here. For instance, a gender identity disorder, such as effeminacy, is present most of the time independent of sexual excitement; it may be found in both perverse and nonperverse men.

Second, whether an aberration is a variant or a perversion is determined by one's attitude toward the object of one's excitement. If one's choice of this object—man, woman, dog, part of the body, inanimate thing, whatever —is motivated by the desire to harm the object and is sensed as an act of revenge, then the act is perverse.

Third, every time the perverse act is performed with others or privately in masturbation, a triumph is celebrated.

Fourth, the trauma of childhood mentioned in the definition actually occurred and is memorialized in the details of the perversion. My hypothesis is that a perversion is the reliving of actual historical sexual trauma aimed precisely at one's sex (an anatomical state) or gender identity (masculinity or femininity),* and that in the perverse act the past is rubbed out. This time, trauma is turned into pleasure, orgasm, victory. But the need to do it again—unendingly, eternally again in the same manner—comes from one's inability to get completely rid of the danger, the trauma. It happened; and, except at the moment when the act of perversion has pro-

*Valenstein says the trauma may not have been experienced literally but may have been an "experiential misconception" of a real event (114, p. 9).

gressed smoothly, one cannot make out to oneself, even though the memory is unconscious, that it did not happen. We do not need a steamy construct like "repetition compulsion" to explain the repeating; in perversion, one repeats because repeating now means that one will escape the old trauma and because revenge and orgasm deserve repeating. Those are reasons enough.

From Freud on, it has been said that precocious excitement contributes to perversion. I would agree, but only —as must usually be the case—when there has been too much stimulation and too little discharge or severe guilt. These will then be sensed as traumatic and will need to be transformed via the magic of the perverse ritual into a successful venture. With much gratification and little guilt at too young an age, on the other hand, I think the result is not perversion but aberration, a holding on, into adult life, to that deviant way of getting pleasure, which is not driven, as is perversion, by the need to harm an object.

Fifth, one has to ensure, over the years of trial and error in constructing fantasies, that one finally arrives at a rendering—the adult perversion—that works smoothly. One's failure in construction is marked on one side by lack of sexual interest—boredom—and on the other by anxiety. Both are manifested in disturbed potency. If the daydream is to work, the story must not arouse too much anxiety, which in unadulterated form is the enemy of pleasure. But one must reduce anxiety without also ending excitement. This is done by introducing a sense of risk into the story. A *sense* of risk; in reality, the risk cannot be great or anxiety will arise. One can only have the impression of risk.

This requires a few words now and in case material later. There are sexual acts in which gross risk-taking is essential: for instance, hanging oneself to achieve orgasm. What we must distinguish, however, is that the risk buried among the fantasies of the sexual act is not the same as that which threatens in the real world; the risk from the noose—death—is not the risk—anxiety or guilt —that fantasy must avoid.

Sixth, the result of all this work of constructing the fantasy we know as the perversion is that one's sex objects are dehumanized. This is obvious in, say, fetishism or necrophilia. But look closely at cryptoperversions such as rape, or a preference for prostitutes, or compulsive promiscuity (Don Juanism or nymphomania), which the naïve observer may see only as heterosexual enthusiasms: in fact the object is a person with a personality, while the perverse person sees a creature without humanity—just an anatomy or clichéd fragments of personality (for example, "what a piece of ass," "all men are brutes"). This is hardly a new idea. In 1930, E. Straus noted: "The delight in perversions is caused by . . . the destruction, humiliation, desecration, the *deformation* of the perverse individual himself and of his partner" (Straus's italics).*

But these propositions do not tell how pleasure is introduced. If perversion is the result of threat and the resultant hatred, whence comes pleasure? Unmitigated trauma or frustration has no lust in it, nor does rage. Pleasure is released only when fantasy—that which makes perversion uniquely human—has worked. With fantasy, trauma is undone, and in the daydream—the manifest content, the conscious, constructed story line of fantasy—it can be undone, over and over as necessary.

In redoing the world, daydreams contribute to pleasure first by ridding one of fear of the trauma being repeated. Second, the daydream has in it elements that simulate risk, so that excitement—tension—is introduced. Third, the daydream guarantees a happy ending, saying that this time one has not only surmounted the trauma but even thwarted if not traumatized those who

*E. Straus, *Geschehnis und Erlebnis* (Berlin, 1930), p. 113. Quoted in 7, p. 20.

were the original attackers. Finally, when the daydream becomes attached to genital excitement and especially to orgasm, the "rightness" of the daydream is reinforced and the person motivated to repeat the experience under like circumstances.

Another problem: if perversion is erotized hatred, why (except for homosexuality) is perversion found more in males? If it is erotized hatred, then we will have to find hatred more—or in different form—in men than in women. This may be so. We shall study it further (chap. 8).

In order to begin to judge these ideas, draw on your own experience. Think of perversions with which you are familiar: necrophilia, fetishism, rape, sex murder, sadism, masochism, voyeurism, pedophilia—and many more. In each is found—in gross form or hidden but essential in the fantasy—hostility, revenge, triumph, and a dehumanized object. Before even scratching the surface, we can see that someone harming someone else is a main feature in most of these conditions. Later on we shall test these ideas harder by looking at conditions in which this mechanism is less manifest; we shall find that it still takes little clinical skill—or theory-making—to find the hostility mechanism. We shall also see the perverse act thread its way between anxiety and boredom in a search for the right sort of risk to create excitement.

It is too bad that my attempt to define fails to extricate us from an old problem: I cannot state how much perversion is needed before we can diagnose the condition as a perversion (just as there is no precise measure in, say, anxiety neurosis for the amount of anxiety that must be present, and no precise point at which character structure becomes character disorder). The demand is an artificial one, however; diagnosis in medicine is no more than a convenience, an effort to convey as much information as possible in the fewest words about the clinical features, underlying pathodynamics, and etiology.

Those of us who are psychiatrists all went to medical school, so we long for a diagnostic system that will communicate as well as that which covers most of the disorders other physicians study. And if the psychiatrist is like the sex researchers in that he does not believe there are psychic states that originate in conflict and are maintained by mental mechanisms like fantasy, repression, undoing, and splitting, he will keep pressing for psychiatric diagnoses that are as tidy as, say, "compound comminuted fracture of the femur," "appendicitis," or "rabies."

It does not work. Our classification uses too many different methods to arrive at a diagnosis. In other words, the rationales for making a diagnosis slip and slide from category to category, revealing that makeshift convenience, more than logic or data, controls the arrangement. Without effort I can think of a number of unrelated ways currently used for diagnosing, and you can easily add more.

1. *Diagnosis as it is employed in the rest of medicine;* examples are "autosomal trisomy of group G" or "psychosis with brain trauma."

2. *A syndrome;* an example is the label "schizophrenia," which most of us feel is actually a group of conditions with different etiologies, courses, and prognoses.

3. *An outstanding symptom* (regardless of the underlying character structure and the other neurotic symptoms also present); examples are "anxiety neurosis" or "phobic neurosis."

4. *An outstanding sign* (ditto 3); examples are "homosexuality" or "fetishism."

5. *A single symptom;* examples are "tic" or "speech disturbance."

6. *A single sign;* examples are "enuresis" or "encopresis."

7. *A chronic way of life;* examples are "paranoid personality" or "inadequate personality."

8. *Body-organ pathology due in part to mental states;* an example is "psychophysiologic skin disorder."

9. *Drug dependence;* examples are "alcohol addiction" or "drug dependence, heroin."

10. *Potpourri;* examples are "social maladjustment" or "marital maladjustment."

This is a system?

If the diagnosis in most cases gives only the illusion of exactness, it will be safer for us to make do with simple descriptions that summarize the observable; we can manage that way right now, and we will not be forced to do the impossible—to measure if someone is perverse enough to be labeled as having a perversion. Our work will not suffer; we will still be able to make our usual wise or foolish decisions about, say, treatment or criminality.

The definitions outlined here need extended discussion; but before looking more closely at the differences between "variant" and "perversion," I want to consider recent sex research against the background of traditional psychoanalytic findings and theory that have dominated ideas about sexual behavior for several generations.

Chapter 2

Impact of New Advances in Sex Research on Psychoanalytic Theory

Psychoanalytic theory is Freud's creation; most modifications introduced by others have not only been minor but are elaborations of theoretical positions he had already explicitly introduced. Therefore this chapter will examine the sexual theories of Freud alone. While one cannot usually discuss any sector of his work without remembering how it changed as the years passed, this is less true for his sexual theories.

Reviewing these theories, one recognizes that Freud did not clarify what he meant by "sexuality," and so at times his discussion was blurred. If one is searching for explanations that cover a universe, then systematic precision may be an encumbrance; but for our present needs, it will help to note different areas of observation or discourse covered by "sex," "sexual," and "sexuality." Certainly, recent research has assumed that the following are distinct.

First, "sexual" for Freud meant any attribute of living tissue expressing negative entropy; he called this *libido*, a mystical tendency toward being alive, staying alive, and reproducing livingness.

Next, there are biological attributes that define an organism as male or female; these can be genetic, anatomical, or physiological. In themselves, they usually have no psychological connotation, though Freud's predilection for biologizing had him reading primeval psychological motivation (for example, life versus death instincts) into such mechanistic processes as cell function and even molecular chemistry.

Next, "sexual" described the same experiences that others called "sensual"; if an activity brought body pleasure, that pleasure was to be labeled "sexual" because Freud found in infants' first experiences of pleasure from birth on the origins of the later activities that all recognize as erotic.

Next, "sexual" meant masculinity and femininity.

Next, it referred to reproductive behavior.

And finally, "sexual" meant erotic, that is, intense sensations in various parts of the body, especially the genitals, which are accompanied by fantasies (conscious or unconscious) of intimacy with other objects, creating a desire for genital satisfaction.

With connotations as broad as this, covering all activities and tendencies of living tissues, we are in trouble if our discussion is not confined to the more habitually accepted meanings of "sexual." This has practical value, keeping my presentation within bounds; and we are also forced to such a strategy because the grander and more mystical a piece of Freud's theory is, the less likely it is that any research procedure can be developed to test it.

So let us focus this discussion almost completely on the two areas of behavior for which the term "sexual" is commonly used: the search, originating in the drive toward reproduction, for erotic pleasure, and the development and maintenance of masculinity and femininity.

Another few orienting remarks. Brought up in a great neurophysiological tradition, yet by nature speculative, Freud was forever drawn to the mind-body problem. A fine observer, perhaps the greatest naturalist of human behavior ever, he was also at least as much enthralled by biological speculation. He wished to bridge the gap between the findings of biology, both experimental and natural, and that mysterious product of neurophysiology, the mind. His unending ruminations on instinct—a term he used to bridge that gap—are evidence. So, if he was to solve this problem, his search might well place him from the start in the issues of sexuality, where body and mind seem so patently to interact ("The concept of instinct is thus one of those lying on the frontier between the mental and the physical" [24, p. 168]). That same search had him extending the meaning of "sexuality" more and more as the years passed, till he made it synonymous with "life." He let a word—"instinct"—do the work that would better have been attempted by scientific methodology: observation followed by controlled attempts to confirm. (Whether the mind-body problem can ever be solved, even whether there is such a problem in reality, is still uncertain.) Of course, he realized early on that neurophysiological knowledge was too rudimentary and deferred his hopes for these data to the future. We can take pleasure in our fantasy that the new advances in sex research would have pleased Freud; he was never one long to flinch at new findings or at giving up old positions.

My presentation is based on five concepts of sexuality that run through Freud's writings from almost the beginning of his great work—just before and after 1900—to his death, and I shall test each one against recent advances in sex research. The five concepts are bisexuality, infantile sexuality and the oedipus complex, libido theory, the primacy of the penis, and conflict. While each is interwoven with the others in making up Freud's coherent theory of sexuality, I shall separate them for ease of discussion. In doing so, I shall emphasize the impact more than the details of the "new advances."

Constitutional Bisexuality

Freud felt there is a biological substrate—the "bed-rock" (34)—of bisexuality,* upon which all later psychological development is anchored. His support for this thesis came from sources as outlandish as Fliess's theory of periodic numbers that control human fate (28 for females and 23 for males) to the sound embryological studies that demonstrated rudiments of one sex within the other. In the monumental *Three Essays on the Theory of Sexuality* (1905), he laid out the fundamental rule from which he never turned: "Since I have become acquainted with the notion of bisexuality I regarded it the decisive factor, and without taking bisexuality into account, I think it would scarcely be possible to arrive at an understanding of the sexual manifestations that are actually to be observed in men and women" (24, p. 220). Henceforth, it was a biological given, for which he demanded no further evidence.

Biological bisexuality was thus considered the anlage of the psychological bisexuality Freud felt was present in all humans. He (and those classical analysts who most closely followed him) found bisexuality—or more accurately, fear of it—etiological in the psychoses, the neuroses, the perversions, the addictions—in all forms of psychopathology, and finally in all normal development. It lay at the root of all symptoms and all behavior. In his last great paper, *Analysis Terminable and Interminable* (1938), he still found it crucial. At the end of this paper, as if to sum up all the rest, he said: "We often have the impression that with the wish for a penis [in females] and the masculine protest [in males] we have penetrated

---

*He uses "bisexuality" in several ways, ignoring distinctions so as to arrive at the highest level of abstraction. Thus we are often uncertain if he means a prime principle of all living cells, a state of anatomical affairs in the embryo, anal pleasure in the child, friendship in people of the same sex, overt homosexuality, or a universal attribute of human sexuality. He felt they were all aspects of the same phenomenon; I do not.

through all the psychological strata and have reached bedrock, and that thus our activities are at an end. This is probably true, since, for the psychical field, the biological field does in fact play the part of the underlying bedrock" (34, p. 252).

Where are we nowadays with this concept that there is a biological bisexuality, and where are we with the related idea that such a "force" is an essential effector of human behavior, normal and pathological? I think most analysts today believe in something like Freud's biological bisexuality (now more stylishly called "sexual bipotentiality" or "sexual dimorphism"): we know that cells, tissues, and organs in each sex can be modified in the direction of the opposite sex. Most of us, however, would not look on these findings as indicating bisexuality quite as Freud understood the term.

Especially following Jost's embryological work (recently reviewed in [71]), the evidence has piled up that in mammals anatomical and physiological maleness does not ever occur, regardless of chromosomal sex (XX in females, XY in males), unless the fetus secretes male hormones (apparently initiated by the Y chromosome). Even, and especially, the brain requires such masculinization in mammals or else femininity will result.

That humans share in the general rule of the femaleness of mammalian tissue seems borne out when we look at the "natural experiments" of endocrine disorders. There we see in each instance that the fetus that is deprived of androgen at critical times in its development fails to show anatomic maleness. For instance, the XO (Turner's syndrome) infant, whatever her defects, has no male tissues, for she has no gonad to produce androgen, and in the androgen insensitivity syndrome, the inability of target tissues to respond to circulating androgens restrains fetal development to femaleness. On the other hand, the female fetus that is exposed to increased androgen, as in hyperadrenalism, is masculinized, and in the extreme case, the clitoris is anatomically indistinguishable from a penis.

But those examples teach us about anatomy; none of this per se touches on psychoanalytic theories of behavior, except to indicate, as Freud had already been taught, that the male organism's tissues can be as if female, and vice versa for females. Freud's interest as a psychologist was not in these anatomic matters but in the mind-body problem. How do these physiological states affect behavior? Here we are especially indebted to John Money, whose studies on people with such endocrine disorders as those noted above suggest that the fetal human brain also needs to be "primed" with androgen for normal masculine development, and that if the female fetal brain is exposed to androgens, a mild though measurable increase in masculine behavior in the growing girl can be expected as compared with control females (108). Other studies suggest that an unusual number of males with congenital hypogonadism, and thus, presumably, inadequate fetal androgen (for example, Klinefelter's syndrome), are feminine in behavior from earliest childhood on, regardless of rearing (110, 137).

Recent reports have suggested that homosexuality in males is caused primarily by biological forces. Geneticists have argued that homosexuality is inherited (72, 128). One worker has described instant cure of homosexuality by neurosurgical means (coagulation of Cajal's nucleus in the ventromedial hypothalamus), indicating a precise brain center for the behavior (122, 9). Other studies have shown decreased plasma testosterone levels and impaired spermatogenesis (83) and abnormal androsterone/etiocholanalone ratio (98) in direct relation to degree of homosexuality. No one of these studies contradicts the others; they may be measuring different aspects of the same process: genes, neuroanatomy, or chemistry. (They may also be flat-out wrong in their conclusions.) And none necessarily contradicts psychoanalytic theory, if each is a piece of the underlying "bed-rock" to which Freud referred. However, if the claim is made that these biological mechanisms are *the* cause of homosexuality, then of course Freud's theory of disturbed interpersonal relationships (oedipal and preoedipal conflict) is in doubt.

But these physiological studies, animal or human, do not explicate human sexual behavior; they only tell us about underlying biological *potentialities*, as do so many other studies in regard to an aspect of human behavior. (An epileptic seizure tells us something about aggression and violence, as does a decorticated cat, but it does not tell all.) As usual, what is made of those potentialities usually lies in the area of environmental influences. For help in this regard, let us turn to the theories of interpersonal, object relations and of social learning.

Infantile Sexuality and the Oedipus Complex

Freud believed bisexuality (and all sexuality) arises from two sources. The first is biological, as we have already seen. This produces an unalterable part of human psychology, which leads in men to a fear of not being manly and in women an urge to be manly. The second is environmental.

> It is not possible to adopt the view that the form to be taken by sexual life is unambiguously decided, once and for all, with the inception of the different components of the sexual constitution. On the contrary, the determining process continues. [24, p. 237] . . . the constitutional factor must await experiences before it can make itself felt; the accidental factor must have a constitutional basis in order to come into operation. To cover the majority of cases we can picture what has been described as a "complemental series" in which the diminishing intensity of one factor is balanced by the increasing intensity of the other; there is, however, no reason to deny the

existence of extreme cases at the two ends of the series.
[p. 239]

By "the accidental factor" he means environmental experience, and he is saying here what most of us believe: the importance of the biological or the environmental in determining sexual behavior varies from person to person and from one time to the next. Feeling that all his psychoanalytic theories were ultimately biological, he did not adequately differentiate between biological philosophizing and the rigors of biological research. The former should be ignored (although, unfortunately, it has been the basis of the fiercest battles inside psychoanalysis, for example, the concept of psychic energy, life versus death instinct, libido theory, Lamarckian inheritance of past experiences of the human race) unless analysts are also willing to do the scientific work necessary to defend these theories.

In fact, on putting aside Freud's "biologizing," we find his contributions, now standing clear, perhaps even more formidable. One of the greatest of these has been his emphasis on infantile and childhood sexuality. He underlined the crucial importance of parent-child relationships (we shall look at that shortly when discussing the oedipus complex) as a cornerstone of his work almost from the start. What Freud undertook, as early as 1900 (23), was the most powerful and explanatory social learning theory of human development ever proposed.

Over the decades, his biological speculations have not been confirmed. However, his interpersonal theories and his observations of parent-child interactions, many fundamentals of which have not been refuted, have been a rich source for innumerable researchers to the present (including many who, to their shame, refuse to acknowledge his gift to them).

Freud told us, as no one had before, that parents have the greatest possible influence on their children's devel-

opment, that children create psychic structure in response, that adult sexual life can be traced back to effects
in infancy, and that sexual desire and gratification have
origins in infancy, long before their obvious upsurge at
puberty. Exactly how parents transmit these influences
to their children has been the subject of increasing study
by analysts and nonanalysts for years. Freud's ideas
spurred the researches of physiologists, behaviorists,
ethologists, general systems theorists—innumerable
workers who now believe infancy and childhood are crucial developmental phases.

Social learning theorists, as they are called in academic
circles, or object relations theorists, as they are known
among psychoanalysts, have, of course, great theoretical
differences. These may obscure an overriding similarity:
the belief that behavior can be radically modified solely
by the effects of one person on another. These workers
also share the belief that the personality of the infant and
small child, more than that of the adult, is especially
vulnerable to permanent behavior modification. Their
major area of disagreement may be over the question
whether trauma, conflict, defense, and compromise formation as a resolution of conflict contribute fundamentally to personality formation.

We must here separate out the two different aspects of
sexuality presented earlier. The first is that concerned
with genital pleasure, more or less tied to reproductive
behavior or its avoidance, and the other is gender behavior, that related to masculinity and femininity. Here
again I wish to emphasize the danger of extrapolating
from animal to human behavior, even if such caution is
currently unfashionable. Of all the areas of behavior in
which there is discontinuity between animals, even pri-
mates, and man, the greatest is in motivated behavior.
The evolutionary rule is not only that certain fundamental behaviors persist, tied to neuroanatomic structures
and circuits that are constant across species, but also that

the higher one goes in the evolutionary scale, the greater the amount of choice available to the organism.

The brain substrates of what we call "choice" or "freedom" simply do not exist in any other creature as in man. No one seriously questions that man's potential for variability of behavior is greater than that of any other animal or that man's behavior, even in its neurophysiological roots, requires more priming (organization) by environment. For instance, we can search the evolutionary scale forever to find biological roots for aggression, but we cannot determine from that source why man so easily murders his own kind. Perhaps someday we shall find a thalamic focus for penile erections in man such as exists in monkeys (89); that sort of behavior—the fundament—obeys evolutionary rules. But there is a whole other level of behavior that is much more complicated, though the final action is simple and physiological—say, erection. The input leading to this latter behavior is not only thalamic or hypothalamic but goes through the unknown neurophysiology that is the result of previous experience fixed in memory and modified by fantasy (especially unconscious fantasy). It is unique to man. Man remembers differently from other animals: *he symbolizes and he fantasies,* and in that way he not only remakes the past but invents the future he anticipates.

In closer relation to our subject, an evolutionary perspective has failed to teach us much about human sexual desires, object choices, or pathology. For instance, the perversions, with their habitual, driving need for aberrant genital satisfaction, are not found in free-ranging members of lower species, but they are ubiquitous in man. The puny attempts to demonstrate perversion in lower animals (for example, the assertion that cows that mount other females are homosexuals) are not edifying.

Similarly, studies that reveal the distortions of behavior that can be permanently built into animals by experiments (such as conditioning, imprinting, or implanting electrodes in discrete brain structures) tell us about potentialities but do not give us answers about free-ranging behavior in man; the data only show us more questions we should ask. In other words, these findings in animals confirm nothing about humans; they only suggest. It is important for analysts, however, to recognize that, when theory-building, they ignore such suggestions at their peril.

For Freud, sexual development depends powerfully on relationships between parents and their child—the oedipus complex. Let us quickly review this hypothesis.

First, masculinity. The infant male, blessed with his inherently superior biological state, starts life as a heterosexual, says Freud. From the moment he becomes a separate being—the moment of birth—the first object of his awareness, intimacy, need, and love is a person of the opposite sex, a female, his mother. Becoming aware of the world around him and of his own body, he recognizes that his penis is a source of intense sensations and serves as the prime evidence of his maleness and therefore his superiority. This may even be reinforced by an inherited, unconscious sense of primacy. He shortly learns by observation (and perhaps, again inherently, even as part of the wisdom of the collective unconscious) that he is different from another group called females. By this point in infancy, then, he prizes his maleness. As his body develops, he reaches a phase in which his penis is the focus of intense erotic sensation. This excitement and its demand for gratification are inextricably linked with his first and continuing love object, his mother, and so he wishes to take his father's place in her life. However, being small and vulnerable, he cannot do so, for his powerful father blocks the way. Any hopes he has of possessing his mother are dashed by the threat of castration and its inevitable consequent anxiety. And so, over a period of several years, he struggles to control his oedipal wishes, and will succeed, without severe damage to masculinity, if he can learn that his sexual wishes for his mother can be deferred, to be played out on another female later in life. Although a rival in this struggle, his father also becomes his ally by serving as a model for masculinity and encouraging the boy to emulate masculine behavior, as long as it does not include possession of his mother.

The course of the little girl's gender development is, according to Freud, more circuitous. He says that she starts with a homosexual relationship, for her first love is a female. The second obstacle athwart her development is her discovery that there are people—males—with a superior sexual apparatus, and so in earliest childhood the girl is envious at not being a male and blames her mother for this deprivation. In fact, some girls believe they were not simply deprived but that they had this possession at an earlier time and were then robbed of it. If she is to become feminine, therefore, the girl must give up her hopes of ever being a male (or her fantasy that she once was one) and, resigned to this defeat, embark on a new path, femininity. To the extent she can do so she will transfer her love from the first, homosexual object to her father. In good part this process can succeed only if the girl gives up her fixation on her clitoris, which she sees only as a little penis. This becomes possible if she turns to her father in the hope that he can give her the ideal replacement for a penis, namely, a baby. If she can fantasy that this is so, she eventually becomes vaginally responsive, but that this is an uncertain process is demonstrated by the large number of women who depend on clitoral orgasm. Mature female sexuality, part of which is femininity, is therefore marked, says Freud, by the capacity for vaginal orgasm, and those women who cannot manage this are by definition unfeminine, appearances, interests, or fantasy life to the contrary.

The oedipus situation is therefore the crux of gender

development. In the boy, masculinity results only if he successfully surmounts the dangers of imagined castration by his father, while in the girl the development of femininity precedes the oedipal conflict and is essential for it to occur; only when the girl becomes feminine does she give up her attachment to her mother and attempt to reach her father. This is then thwarted by her mother, who once again becomes villainous (the first time was in depriving the girl of her penis). Therefore the little girl, like the little boy, will, if successful, defer her complete heterosexuality until she is older and able to focus it on a different man from her father. Thus, masculinity in boys requires successful resolution of the oedipal situation, and femininity in girls requires only the arrival at the start of the oedipal conflict.

Because Freud saw this process as more conflict-laden and devious in girls, he felt he had an explanation for his conviction that adult female sexuality is less certain, less gratifying, and more mysterious than that of males. A curious addition to his theory was his belief that the development of little boys and little girls is about the same until the onset of the full-blown development of the oedipal situation at around five or six years, and that therefore no significant, true femininity is present in little girls younger than this. "Both sexes seem to pass through the early phases of libidinal development in the same manner. . . . With their entering into the phallic phase the differences between the sexes are completely eclipsed by their agreement. We are obliged now to recognize that the little girl is a little man" (33, pp. 117–118).

Some workers (for example, Malinowski [97]) have claimed that the oedipus complex is imaginary because its form is different in some societies, as in those where the genetic father's place as the psychological father is taken by one of the mother's kin. But so far, there are no descriptions of cultures in which the growing child does not look upward toward a large and powerful male who serves as a model for masculinity in boys and a model heterosexual object for girls, or toward a female who mothers. What varies from family to family and culture to culture is how much conflict there is in the complex, but not whether families are made up of mothers, fathers, and children each with attributes of power and sex more or less as Freud noted in Vienna.

Where at present is this theory of the development of masculinity and femininity? A new factor has been thrown into the discussion by studies on the earliest stages of gender development, which contradict Freud in several places. It has been found that certain boys, because of an oddity in child-rearing practices, are markedly feminine from their earliest days on. They have spent excessive time in intense, blissful intimacy with their mothers, and the mothers who are more likely be this close to their sons are drawn to marry distant and passive men. In general, the purer the form this constellation takes in a family, the earlier and the more ingrained and irreversible is the femininity that develops in the boy (142). On the other hand, boys who have close relationships with their fathers are found not to have mothers like this, and these boys are masculine (4).

A girl who has a distant, unloving mother but whose father is close to her develops masculinity if her father encourages her to have the same interests he does (141). A girl whose mother enjoys having a daughter and is not ashamed that her daughter has a female body and whose father encourages his daughter's femininity will grow up feminine (80).

Whether the communications between each parent and the infant mold the child's behavior by imprinting, classical or operant conditioning, identification, or combinations of all these is still to be thrashed out. What is demonstrated in study after study, however, is that attitudes passing between parent and infant are powerfully

instrumental in creating masculinity and femininity in
both sexes. This reduces the conflict (castration anxiety)
aspect of gender development; in contrast to Freud's
theory, in this description conflict-free development also
plays a prominent part.

A greater disagreement with classical analytic theory
arises here. While it is obvious enough that the boy's first
love object is a female (his mother), in his earliest stages
of life a great physical and emotional intimacy (merging)
between him and his mother's body and psyche introduces the risk of a sense of oneness with a female. And
so, one of the boy's first tasks on the way to masculinity
is to separate himself from his mother (chap. 8); that
process can be subverted by a too intimate mother. The
same intimacy does not thus endanger the little girl, for
such closeness with her mother only encourages her
femininity.

New data are appearing in regard to the differential
handling of male and female infants by their mothers
(13); in the usual case (which is more likely to produce
femininity in girls and masculinity in boys), girls have
more contact, physical and visual, with their mothers
during the early months than boys (48). Mothers generally feel easier being intimate with their infant girls than
with their boys. So, the boy does not have the straightfor-
ward heterosexual development Freud alleged. Instead,
he has a major impediment on the way to heterosexuality: he must rid himself of whatever femininity he may
develop in the mother-infant symbiosis. Only then, at a
later stage, can he see his mother as the separate and
desirable object of the classical oedipal situation (26).

And so, rather than girls being little boys, these data
would predict that little girls are shaped in the direction
of femininity right from the start. And that is what simple
observation reveals: girls in general just are not masculine in early childhood. Clear-cut femininity is routinely
seen by a year or so of age; there is no evidence that this

is a façade or an imitation of femininity. Thus I cannot agree with Freud's statement: "As we all know, it is not until puberty that the sharp distinction is established between the masculine and feminine character" (24, p. 219). We shall look into these issues further (chap. 8).

The Primacy of the Penis

Freud accepted as a given the belief that the superior sex is male. He felt this was a fact established throughout mammalia by males' physical superiority in strength: life-or-death struggles select out males as superior because stronger. This fact, with the penis as its most compelling symbolic representation, was then reflected in mythology, folk tales, institutions of society, artistic productions, religious worship, dreams—everywhere.

In the family, such power was granted to the father not only because custom demanded but also because, from ancient times, it was his accepted responsibility to protect his family from physical danger and to provide food and at least minimal comforts, and because, as the strongest member of the family physically, he had life-and-death control over each member. This power, ultimately derived from the reality of physical strength, was institutionalized in society, from the ruler down into the family.

Freud, coming from a culture in which this authority still manifestly resided in fathers, did not have to question his principle "anatomy is destiny." Any theory, however, in which this idea was an essential building block is weakened if the principle is incorrect.

Freud's enthusiasm for the position that men are superior fitted in with what he considered observable fact: that women are secretive and insincere (24, p. 151), more masochistic (33, p. 116), less self-sufficient (p. 117), more dependent and pliant (p. 117), more envious and jealous (p. 125), have defective superegos

(p. 129) and little sense of justice (p. 134), are more bisexual (p. 113), more narcissistic (p. 132), weaker in social interests (p. 134), have less capacity for sublimating instincts (p. 134), and become more rigid and unchangeable at an earlier age (pp. 134–135). They are intellectually inferior because biologically created for the nonintellectual task of motherhood; they are morally inferior because, already without a penis, they cannot easily be threatened and because they are bound more concretely to the real world and so are less concerned with such aesthetic issues as morality (that is, they obey the command of biology rather than a more ethereal call).

It is a corollary of the thesis of male superiority that the prime feature of maleness, the penis, is a superior organ physically and symbolically—and Freud could point to phallic worship, in its myriad forms, as proof to those who did not listen to the dreams of men and women. In the concept of castration anxiety, he found reason to believe that men considered the penis the prime organ of the race, and in penis envy, he found the proof that women also agreed on the primacy of the penis. That it is visible, can change size, is shaped like a weapon, can penetrate, frightens women, and is a source of such intense sensation from infancy on also demonstrates its superiority. When it is contrasted with the female genitals, the case is again made. The female phallus, the clitoris, is much smaller, is not usually visible, cannot penetrate, has not seized mankind's imagination, is never symbolized or exalted, and—Freud thought—is not a competent source of pleasure. Its significance is further weakened in that it must share its fate with another organ, the vagina, which Freud felt was universally considered an inferior organ: hidden, dark, mysterious, uncertain, unclean, and undependable in bringing pleasure.

That is a lot of evidence; wherever he looked in the

outer world or in mental life, the primacy of the penis seemed proved.

Offered against Freud's argument is the exciting new research alluded to earlier. In mammalian species the function of cells is female in both sexes until androgens are added in fetal life. In fact, except for the chromosomes, one cannot talk about two sexes until the androgens have been added; there is only femaleness. Freud, who always had a nose for mystery and who found so many of his mysteries at the most fundamental levels—cell function or even more primitive—would have been nonplussed by this finding. And he would have been even more disturbed in his argument to learn that this female cast to tissue extends into the central nervous system, where, as has now been demonstrated in mammals other than man, future masculine behavior in the male requires the organizing only androgens produce, while in the female nothing need be added for femininity. So the new research would seem to put Freud's argument in a most precarious position; and since he chose to extend his beliefs from the realm of psychodynamics into morality and other cosmic issues, in the last few years he has been well beaten about the head.

Nonetheless, we ought not yet to find in the new data a proof that mankind does not believe in the primacy of the penis; one can still ask where in the child's psyche resides this knowledge of embryology or tissue capability. It is not to be found. But we can easily detect boys' and girls' attitudes about penises; they still find them impressive. Is this primacy? Some no longer think so, but instead feel it is too bad Freud did not emphasize more strongly that children of both sexes are also deeply stirred by the significance of breasts and womb; reproductive power is more difficult to represent visually, but, if measured by the mystery it creates, is more important even than the penis.

In addition, the observations of Masters and Johnson (102) have had a great effect in diminishing Freud's ideas about femininity. Freud said a girl is masculine until she gives up her hope for a penis; as long as she hopes, she retains her fixation on her clitoris, as if it were a penis. Only if she shifts her erotism to the generative inner space, the vagina and pelvic organs, will she be feminine. But Masters and Johnson have found that all female orgasms originate in the clitoris;* they have not observed vaginal orgasms. So Freud's argument seems disproved.

And I believe it is—but not at all by Masters' and Johnson's work. Innumerable women have sensed that they have two sorts of orgasms, one clitoral, the other vaginal; they have no trouble distinguishing the two. Just because gross vaginal changes at the moment of orgasm are not visible to these observers, this does not prove the absence of vaginal orgasm. Perhaps its physiology—as can happen with intense pain or itch, in muscle or skin —is only not *grossly* visible; or perhaps vaginal orgasm requires penile intercourse with a meaningful man and is not producible in a laboratory; or perhaps there is so much action in the vagina at the moment of an orgasm produced by penetration that the view is obscured. Their work has not disproved that there is an orgasm experienced deeper in the body than is a clitoral orgasm. So their argument does not dislodge Freud. Another does: too many feminine women have been known who do not have vaginal orgasms (111), and too many women do have them who, by Freud's definition of maturity, cannot be feminine—schizophrenics, neurotics of all types and degrees, and even grossly masculine women.

But this is a nonscientific discussion masked by pseu-

*No one seems to remember that Freud also said this: "When at last the sexual act is permitted [for the first time] and the clitoris itself becomes excited, it still retains a function: the task, namely, of transmitting the excitation to the adjacent female sexual parts, just as— to use a simile—pine shavings can be kindled in order to set a log of harder wood on fire" (24, p. 221).

doscientific rationalization (106, 127). How can one prove one sex superior to the other if one does not first state the categories to be measured? If superiority is measured by body size, phallic dimensions, skill in football, fatherliness, or production of sperm, females are unequivocally inferior; the differences can be measured. Likewise, if superiority is measured by size of bosom, gestational capacity, longevity, resistance to illness, motheringness, or capacity to ovulate, women have a great edge. In the middle lie innumerable skills at which neither men nor women inherently excel, such as weaving, growing rice, solving problems in psychoanalytic research, running an advertising agency, or bickering. And then there are imponderables such as: Is a woman superior if she can have limitless orgasms? Is a man superior if he is completely satisfied after one or five? This sort of foolishness, so intensely argued these days, proves nothing. Instead of pontificating about superiority, we might simply try to observe the development of males and females and masculinity and femininity. Let us relieve ourselves of the burden of deciding which is the better sex.

Libido Theory

Libido theory is part of Freud's generalized theory of instincts. I shall not concern myself here with the scientific and epistemological questions raised over the years about the concept of instinct (or drive); instead, I wish only to discuss libido theory, that description of the maturation of sexuality as a movement and elaboration through stages, each of which has its focus on a different part of the body. Concomitant with his object relations theory, embodied in his description of the oedipus complex, Freud saw a development, governed by an inherited timing mechanism, in which—in all humans— "psychic energy" converges on a part of the body, "cathecting" it with "libido." (I do not have time—seventy years was not enough—to discuss the pros and cons of the concept of "psychic energy," nor need we be concerned here that neither "cathexis" nor "libido" was ever defined in scientific terms.)

The inexorable progress of libidinal development starts with the oral phase, wherein the infant's life-preservative, affectionate, and sensual drives center in the mouth and its functions. Next is the anal phase, with its pleasures of expelling and retaining feces (and urine), and then the phallic phase, in which boy and girl focus on their intense penile or clitoral sensations and note their anatomical differences. The final libidinal phase is genital maturity, consisting of loving and genitally gratifying heterosexual relations, and is reached only by those fortunate few who surmount the oedipal conflict. To this theory of libido, a conceptual groundwork for all human psychology, was added an important corollary, that different emotional disorders took their origin from two sorts of disturbances occurring at one of these libidinal phases: fixation due to excessive gratification during that phase, or regression because of anxiety from a more advanced to an earlier phase. This special theory is mentioned now only because Freud based his theories of the production of perversions particularly on the libido theory's description of sexual advance from zone to zone.

As a description of human childhood development, Freud's observations on zonal phases have been confirmed and can be so any time with biologically normal children. However, no studies have been published that confirm the implications drawn from the observations. It has not yet been shown that any class of neurosis, including perversion, or psychosis is caused by a disruption of the sensual experiences of the mouth, defecatory or urinary systems, or phallus (see, for example, 99, 11). (There is, however, much evidence that disturbed *object relations* during these phases cause psychopathology.) Libido theory as an explanation of neurosogenesis has been so far off base that it has never attracted serious attempts to test it by scientific methods.

An odd piece of libido theory is the notion that libido is a quantitative energy that flows or can be dammed and that the function of the "mental apparatus" is to reduce the "instinctual tension"—unpleasure—that results from such damming. True, people usually get pleasure from tension reduction, as with sleeping, eating, intercourse, excreting, affect discharges, skin scratching, and so forth. But is that an effect of the postulated libido? Being a neurophysiological construct, libido can be challenged by a neurophysiological model. As it turns out, libido is as hard to seize as were the "humors" of past eras. Rather, mammals (113), including man (66), have a precise brain center that produces the subjective experience called pleasure. Experimentally, it does not deplete as if drained. It can be turned on and off endlessly, so that an animal can experience the same degree of intense pleasure even thousands of times an hour (113). Even the most parsimonious explanation of pleasure at present does not resemble this hydraulic model of a flow of substance or energy; the energic requirements of a central nervous system switching mechanism are infinitesimal.

Conflict

Two types of painful situations can influence personality development and thus sexual development. First there are traumas (acute, chronic, or cumulative), severe impingements on the infant by events not felt as emanating from its own psyche. These events may be unpleasant internal sensations, such as hunger, body pain, or respiratory distress, or they may be external struggles against objects separate from one's body that frustrate or traumatize—inanimate objects intermittently and important people persistently, especially mother at first. Not all traumas produce conflict; the second category of painful situations, conflict, implies intrapsychic struggle in order to *choose* among possibilities. Thus, if a small child has a powerful sensual impulse that is forbidden by his parent, this does not cause *intra*psychic conflict even though the child may change his outward behavior when the parent punishes him. Later in childhood, however, if the parents' value system has been learned and accepted (internalized) by the child, there will be present within the psyche a set of moral positions received from the parents plus an inner technique of self-punishment based on guilt. This then exemplifies intrapsychic conflict: one part of oneself threatening or punishing another part, frustrating the latter's drive toward a gratification.

Trauma or frustration may cause reaction (change) rather than conflict. For instance, early in infantile development a stimulus may produce change without conflict by an ethological process like imprinting, by classical conditioning, or by operant conditioning. (These participate in creating such nonconflictual behavior as modes of speech or preferences in toys, clothes, or food.) Freud did not believe trauma caused perversion of sexual development until it caused conflict; conflict is awareness of the need to choose between alternatives and requires a development advanced enough that memory, judgment, and perhaps fantasy are beginning to influence behavior. He seems to leave no room for the idea of a sexual aberration that is not also a perversion, that is, a habitual aberrant erotic act not the product of conflict: "We were thus led to regard any established aberration from normal sexuality as an instance of developmental inhibition and infantilism" (24, p. 231). For him, all sexual aberration resulted from fixations and traumas at the various stages of childhood libidinal development, with the threats and punishments surrounding desire for parents—the oedipal conflict—as the decisive factors.

Freud's theory of the causes of perversion (as of all sexuality) is a combination of the five categories we have been considering: bisexuality, oedipus complex, the primacy of the penis, libido theory, and conflict. Granted variably powerful constitutional influences, such as inherited bisexual tendencies or unusual constitutional capacity for pleasurable sensation in a nongenital part of the body, he felt that, above all else, it was infantile conflict—castration anxiety, preoedipal and oedipal conflict, fear of heterosexuality—that changed normal sexuality into perversion. In briefest summary, he believed that perversion in males was due to the boy's fear that his desire for his mother could lead to his father cutting off his prized penis, which would make the boy the same as a girl: inferior anatomically and psychically because of castration. In the girl, perversion was said to result from the inability to come to terms with the fact that she is already castrated; she must deny that fact by overemphasizing the value of her clitoris, which prevents her from shifting to the more feminine vagina or makes her unwilling to turn to her father—to heterosexuality. Without taking her father as her new love object (renouncing her mother), she fails to enter into the oedipal conflict as a feminine person who wants to be made whole by a baby. Perversion may mark failure at any step in the process of oedipal development in boys and girls. (In addition to this oedipal [interpersonal] theory, Freud felt that specific elements in perverse acts are the result of libidinal fixation. By this, he meant that when the child's further development was blocked by castration anxiety, the boy or girl might fall back on earlier libidinal gratifications. If, for any reason, mouth, anus or bowel, urethra, skin, or any other body part had been the focus of intense libidinal excitement earlier, the child could regress to this safer and more gratifying "position" in the face of severe anxiety. This accounted, for instance, for anal intercourse among male homosexuals or oral intercourse in male or female homosexuals.)

Sexual aberration leading to orgasm is almost never seen in animals (unless they have been manipulated by unnatural forces like experimentation or captivity). On the other hand, such needs are ubiquitous in man; erotic deviance is as specially human as are murder, humor, fantasy, competitive sports, art, or cooking. This observation is so grossly manifest that one wonders why it has no force in the speculations of modern sex researchers. *Almost every notable study on human sexual behavior since Freud has tried to prove that a person does not create his own deviance* but rather it is thrust on him—by genes, by hormones, by electrical circuiting in the brain, by imprinting, by conditioning, by statistics. How Freud has disturbed us; we still cannot bear his "accusation" that we are human.

Will someone please explain pedophilia in geneticists' terms? Or shoe fetishism as the product of a brain mechanism constant through evolutionary development? Or penile exhibitionism as a hormonal defect? Or the need to rape old women as the effect of conditioning? Or necrophilia as merely a statistic at the outer reaches of a bell curve?

The new research, which takes place in the physiology and chemistry laboratories, in the intact animal and human experiments, and in naturalistic observation, seems aimed unanimously at tearing down the conflict theory; no other aspect of Freud's system has created such resistance, perhaps because Freud believed perversion is *motivated,* that is, a person somehow, in his depths, feels in part responsible for his perversion. The sexual act, Freud felt, is the product of the great human capacity for choice and so ultimately has a moral quality (even if one's responsibility is mitigated since the choice is unconscious and was arrived at because of unsought threatening circumstances in childhood). The modern researchers, however, deny that intrapsychic conflict plays a part or that fantasy propels and perpetuates aberrant activity. In other words, these critics say it is not psychically motivated. Oddly, their research can also apply to nondeviant behavior, for their logic says that *all* sexual behavior is *not* psychically motivated. They believe this in their laboratories and at their desks. Do they also believe it in bed?

The attack on conflict theory has taken four forms. The first says that the aberrations in humans are due simply to physiological mechanisms—either organic dysfunction or inherited normal physiology that merely produces behavioral variance similar to that seen in lower animals and resulting from the same brain and hormonal mechanisms. In the second explanation—learning theory—the deviation is inflicted by an outside force, such as conditioning, and so is not a matter of choice and has no origin in fantasy. The third is statistical: there is a bell curve for sexual behavior and the variations are not abnormal, just not normative. The last says that while cultures may pronounce an aberration pathological, the social condemnation may be all that is pathological, not the behavior; that is, the society, not the individual, is sick.

Genetics and Constitution

The following represents the kinds of studies trying to demonstrate that sexual aberrations are induced by physical, not mental, forces.

There is much fine animal work (summarized in 37 and 140), for now there are techniques to influence large areas of the brain by electrical and chemical stimulation or ablation, or by the deprivation of REM sleep. These experiments create disruptions in normal sexual patterns in animals, hypersexuality or indiscriminate sexual behavior, during which the animal may not care about the sex or sometimes even the species of the object of its attentions. Then there are experiments in which minute electrical or hormonal stimulation of tiny, circumscribed

areas of the brain can change sexual function (104). But
our old problem remains: How do *these* neural substrates
in animals relate to *that* man buying photographs of en-
chained women? Why did *that* woman, who was a feminine girl till age six, grow up to be so masculine?

As yet, obviously, no comparable work has been done
on humans, though we know that sexual behavior can be
changed by brain manipulation (66). I have already mentioned the report of neurosurgical cure of male homosexuality (122). A cure of male homosexuality (85) and
the treatment of hypersexuality (12) by antiandrogens
have been reported. Several reports have tried to impli-
cate the temporal lobes in fetishistic behavior, especially
cross-dressing, but these have either been single cases or
have involved too few subjects (summarized in Blumer,
5), have lacked adequate controls (151), or have simply
been ruminations on research (16). They indicate that a
rare case may be associated with temporal lobe disorder
but do not encourage belief that such brain disorder
underlies all such behavior (145). (Why are there no
reports of females so affected?)

As to the claims that constitutional predisposition may
make certain people susceptible to their particular deviance, there simply is no acceptable evidence as yet, except in the rarest instances (108, 137). No competent
studies have shown family tendencies in any of the perversions, except perhaps in homosexuality. The view
generally held in the early 1900s, that perversion was the
result of "degeneration," meaning some diffuse physical
inferiority, has never been backed up by evidence. But all
studies—and there are very few—that have tried to demonstrate genetic factors in homosexuality (72, 128) have
been unable to withstand the attack of critics so far (reviewed in 73, 101, 115). Even Money's observations of
fetally androgenized females show that the girls become
only mildly masculine in behavior; they are nonetheless
heterosexual (108).

It is too soon to say whether this work on genetics and

brain function tests psychoanalytic theory (though it should result in treatments that would make psychoanalytic therapy obsolete for some sexual disorders). One must always be cautious (as I was not quite when speculating above about the significance of a CNS pleasure center) not to equate the discovery of midbrain mechanisms with discovery of the causes of integrated, motivated human behavior. The limbic substrates for oral and genital behavior lie close together; how many people seriously think that is how man invented oral intercourse? Is the foot center close to the genital center in a foot fetishist? Is masturbation due to activation of a masturbation center in the hypothalamus? I think some of the modern theories were invented by a computer. At the least, it will take a few generations of research on the cortex before we know much about thinking, desire, and behavior; that cortex does not exist in other species.

Perhaps the greatest recent challenge are the reports (noted earlier, in the discussion of bisexuality) which show that the more exclusively homosexual a man, the lower are his testosterone levels and the more defective his spermatogenesis. Such findings, if confirmed, would greatly reduce the importance of a theory that says the condition is caused by disruptions in a boy's relationships with his mother and father. We shall have to await further studies that control for nonspecific influences like stress, normal variations in level during a diurnal cycle, normal variations in semen quantity and content, drug intake (marijuana may lower plasma testosterone levels), and so forth (20, 84). The nonconfirming reports are beginning to outnumber the early challenges (10, 15, 117, 149).

Learning Theory

Learning theorists are the second group whose research opposes the idea that there are sexual aberrations that serve as compromise formations to salvage sexual pleasure from a situation filled with anxiety and conflict. There does not seem to be a learning theory that attempts, as does psychoanalysis, to account for the development of erotic behavior in humans, behavior that leads either to "normal" heterosexuality or to the aberrations. However, there are studies that suggest we may find roots of sexual behavior that are not the result of intrapsychic conflict.

Imprinting of infant creatures at a critical period can cause attachment to an inanimate object, an animal, or a man when they normally would become attached to their mother. In adult life their choice for mating may then be of the type of the imprinted object (87). Although the conceptualizations behind these observations have been extended to the human infant (8, 50, 133), no confirmatory data are yet available.

The contribution that classical conditioning makes to the development of sexual behavior has also been investigated. This can be summarized by saying that, in animals, almost anything is possible in the laboratory: by conditioning techniques, an animal can be trained to become sexually aroused by objects that would have no such power in the natural setting; even styles of gratification, such as masturbation, can be artificially produced. How or whether these findings are related to the development of sexuality in free-ranging conditions is unknown.

"Interpersonal" relations as contributing to the development of sexuality have also been investigated in animals. For instance, overcrowding has produced abnormal effects in animals, changing their object choice and their style, frequency, and capability of intercourse (40). Experiments in which monkeys are raised by abnormal mothers, including inanimate mothers, have caused profound disturbances in socialization and capacity for reproductive behavior (64). Defects in sexual ability also occur when monkeys are deprived of peer relationships when young (63). These studies seem to justify the stress analysts lay on the influence of interpersonal relationships in early life on later sexuality.

My enthusiasm for many fine animal studies is reduced if the author is unable to resist the temptation, on finding an experiment that produces abnormality, to extrapolate directly to human behavior, even to suggesting modifications in child rearing or in the functioning of whole societies, based on findings in, say, rats.

Human conditioning experiments producing sexual behavior are rare. In one, an easily extinguished, mild fetishism was artificially produced by pairing erotically stimulating pictures with shoes (118). Positive and negative reinforcements in a culture may in part account for changing sexual styles from generation to generation (for example, women's fashions).

Social learning theorists stress the effects of shaping—reward and punishment—in creating personality (2, 126), as well as the effects of imitation and identification. Freud and other analysts have also, as in discussions of the development of the ego and superego (21, 31, 65, 94) or core gender identity (137). There are studies on identification wherein some learning theorists and psychoanalysts find common ground. These show that the infant-child who spends considerable time in a close and warm relationship with a parent may pick up the gender qualities of that parent. Thus a boy too close to his mother may be feminized but be masculine when with his father, and vice versa for girls (137, 4). Analysts disagree with most learning theorists in believing personality development does not occur without the influence of intrapsychic conflict over affectionate and sexual issues as well.

"Taxonomy"

The third argument is the statistical one, or, as Kinsey alleged, "taxonomic." (That word was chosen for its implications of objectivity, naturalness, and absence of moral judgments; "normative" is cooler than "normal.") It takes the stance of the naturalist observing humans just as he would another animal species. In Kinsey's hands it became a powerful research tool though also every bit as powerful a hammer of social morality, since in this crafty way Kinsey made a judgment by saying we should be nonjudgmental.

His data (77, 78), and the good subsequent sociological work (such as that by the Kinsey people [41]) have not shaken analytic theory, for they demonstrate what analysts had long since known—that human sexual behavior is far more variable than had been admitted. Kinsey's challenge is not in his data but in the position he took before he even collected any data—that inner life is not pertinent to this psychological research: the observer knows enough when he has finished counting. In that regard, Kinsey is allied with the behaviorists.

Cultural Relativity

The fourth argument extends the third and is exhortative. Here the author uses the research of others to support his position for sexual freedom. This is especially the case with activists banded together to relieve the guilt and social degradation traditionally laid upon them. Homosexuals exemplify this approach, drawing from the first three categories above to deny allegations of abnormality or illness: first, their condition is widespread in lower animals, is inherited, is hormonally or otherwise physiologically induced; or it is the result of conditioning in childhood or adolescence; or it is aberrant only statistically. Crucial for each of these defenses is relief of guilt: since one's self did not choose the condition, one is not responsible for it, and besides it is not shameful.

There is much turmoil today (3, 51, 68, 100, 131) over whether aberrant behavior is perverse (that is, disgusting, sick) or only deviant (statistically askew); the key

words have been "normal" and "healthy." These arguments have been less than inspirational because the con-
tenders, each with Science by his side, have ignored what
the opposition means by "normal" or "healthy." The
one group says the perverse person is abnormal because
the aberrant behavior can be traced back to childhood
trauma and conflict and in the present masks (or may not
even be able to mask) severe psychopathology. The
other says the deviant is not abnormal because he man-
ages his life, other than his personal preferences, no
more peculiarly than heterosexuals, who, anyway, are
not noted in the mass for their happiness and creativity.

I agree with both—and with neither. Many aberrations
are perversions in the sense that they emerge as solutions to conflicts and thus secrete a burden of guilt and
a sense of risk-taking at their core. On the other hand,
I do not believe these dynamics cripple most of their
owners any more than does the conflict-solving that produces normative (heterosexual) behavior. (This is less
true the more bizarre the aberration.) We may not solve
these moral issues, which masquerade as scientific ones,
as easily as each side hopes.

To sum up (and I have reflected on the impact of the
new advances rather than detailing them, and so any
conclusions can only be opinions), I think the measurable impact of this research on psychoanalytic theory has
been mild. First, the theory was drawn up in such a way
that most of it cannot be put as propositions to be tested
by any scientific procedures yet devised. Second, psychoanalysis concerns man, but the new research does not
have the techniques yet to achieve its own primary,
though usually unstated, goal: to show how the findings
of any experiment on animals or on an isolated part of
a human subject's physiology or psychic function bear on
the sexual behavior of a human in his life as a person, not
a laboratory subject. Still, while the measurable impact
on theory has been mild, the impact on analysts may be

considerable. Many are listening closely to the researchers, and into the writings and conversations of analysts is moving an impatience with being confined to theoretical positions glued together more by tradition than by data.

As in many other areas of psychiatric research, new techniques have led to an upsurge of interest in and of findings about the neurophysiological (including chemical) mechanisms involved in many aspects of sexual behavior. Along with this excitement caused by fine experimentation, there is less enthusiasm than ever for investigation of sexuality in the human by clinical methods, especially by collecting data in the supportive environment of proper treatment. I think that nothing but good can come from the increased laboratory work and that nothing but bad can come from ignoring the single case studied in depth.

It will be nice if we can reverse the belief that the clinical method is either so weak (as some laboratory scientists are convinced) or has finished its task (as some psychoanalysts tend to feel). Now, years after the work of such observers as Freud, Krafft-Ebing, or Havelock Ellis, we still need naturalistic observations on sexual behavior, normal and abnormal. The work of Masters and Johnson has convinced us of this. But I am not now referring only to the observation of gross physiological response—which they are doing—but to collecting exact subjective descriptions of the sexual experience, the accompanying fantasies, and the indications of unconscious processes and childhood influences that the psychoanalytic method can gather.

And there may be additional bonuses if we revive clinical research on sexual behavior. For instance, from this neglected area can come great insights into causes of violence, the research of which these days is more to be commended for its volume than its discoveries. It is no coincidence that violently aggressive people usually have bizarre sexual impulses and severe conflicts about masculinity and femininity. And, a second area that sex research may clarify: some legal and moral issues that turn on questions of responsibility and of normality may melt away under the heat of the facts.

Perhaps the group who can give us the most, because (with a few notable exceptions like LaBarre) they have provided the least so far, are the anthropologists. Their acceptance of sketchy, anecdotal material and their failure to develop a method for getting detailed, accurate material on such a private subject as sexual desire have crippled our understanding of human sexuality. We simply cannot do without cross-cultural studies, but we also cannot afford the superficial and opinionated reports they too often have given us. Certainly analysts need their findings to keep us honest, that is, to keep us from generalizing too rapidly from the particular patient we analyze—a member of our culture—to humanity at large.

Finally, it is crucial to remember that we still know very little about the mechanisms or causes of human sexual behavior, normative and variant, normal and abnormal. We still know too little about what affects the unfolding of sexuality after the essential inputs of heredity, constitution, and early environment. We know too little even about what people do, what they think they are doing, what they think while they are doing it, and what they think of what they are doing. However, it may not be too optimistic to say that we are now developing, for the first time, tools and ideas that will enable us to study these issues well.

Chapter 3

Variants: Aberrations That Are Not Perversions

Having oriented the new research to psychoanalytic positions, let us review what evidence there is of a category of aberration that is not perversion. Perhaps a few examples will be enough to make the concept usable. The defining quality in all categories of this group is that, though one finds sexual behavior beyond society's norms, the behavior is not primarily the result of fantasies that are permutations of hostility.

Genetic and Other Constitutional Factors

We have seen (chap. 2) that in both sexes maleness of anatomy occurs only when androgens are added prenatally. Additionally, prenatal hormones organize the brains of all mammals, including humans, in ways that predetermine sexual behavior (both that behavior adding up to erotic experiences—that using the apparatuses of reproduction—and that connected with the nonerotic, nonreproductive behavior called in humans masculinity and femininity). Regardless of whether the organism is genetically male or female, if androgens are not present at the appropriate periods prenatally, masculine behavior will not occur. This has been the invarying rule in innumerable experiments on lower animals and is also confirmed, though less definitively, in "natural experiments" in humans.

In such cases, aberrant erotic or gender behavior is, thus, the result of brain function determined primarily before birth. For instance, women with androgen insensitivity syndrome are chromosomally males, with testes producing testosterone in normal amounts. However, their tissues are unable to respond to testosterone. The external appearance of their bodies is female (the testes being cryptorchid), and they are invariably heterosexual, feminine women (109). Anatomically normal-appearing men with Klinefelter's syndrome (XXY) have an unexpectedly high frequency of disorders of gender identity, from homosexuality through cross-dressing to complete gender reversal with desire for "sex change" surgery. Otherwise genetically and anatomically normal females who have been masculinized *in utero* either by excessive amounts of androgens produced in their adrenals or by progesterone given to their mothers to prevent abortion are more masculine in their interests and behavior than a control group of girls. These, then, are examples of aberrations of sexual behavior in which the dynamics of perversion as defined earlier are not present as a cause.

Postnatal Disorders of Brain Function

There are a handful of cases reported in which aberrant sexual behavior was the result of brain disease. Blumer (5) reviews this meager literature—a few cases of fetishism and cross-dressing in which abnormal temporal lobe foci, sometimes accompanied by the overt manifestations of epilepsy, were found; one case in which a "fetish object (a safety-pin) became the invariable trigger of temporal lobe seizures. . . . During postictal confusion the patient later on occasionally dressed himself in his wife's clothing. A left temporal lobectomy, at age thirty-eight, relieved both the epilepsy and the fetishism"; a series of sixty temporal lobe epileptics with two being homosexual and one with "minimal interest in girls . . . and partial erection by putting on his baby sister's diapers."* Walinder (151) reviews other evidence for cerebral lesions (especially in regard to "transvestism/transsexualism"), including a report in which "transvestism/transsexualism" occurred for the first time in men with senile brain changes.

If an aberration occurs only when brain disorder is present and disappears with treatment of the lesion, there is no point in calling this a perversion, though some do when they try to show that perversions are due to brain, not psychic, dysfunction (16).

Hermaphroditic Identity

Usually, when an infant is born whose genitals appear at birth to be neither unequivocally male nor female, the parents are unable to accept their child as being clearly a male or a female; instead, they feel the child to be in some degree either a mixture of male and female or neither male nor female. A hermaphroditic identity develops, the child believing itself to be of a different sex from the two sexes to which everyone else belongs (134). Such people may then find themselves able to have sexual relations with people of both sexes. But once again, the motivating force for aberrance is not that defined above for perversion but rather results from impulses springing from the bisexual identity, an identity originating in parents teaching their child that it is a hermaphrodite, not from the child's defense against oedipal and preoedipal dangers.

*Since so few are homosexual as compared with the prevalence of homosexuality in the population at large, maybe we can announce from this statistic that temporal lobe disease *protects* against sexual aberration.

Male Transsexualism

The most extreme form of femininity in anatomically intact males is transsexualism, a condition that manifests itself from the earliest years of life with the boy wishing he were a girl, even to having his sex reversed (which he then tries to accomplish later in life). This rare state—and only this condition, which does not include most of those people these days who request "sex change" (139)—is not the result of a lifelong, lived-out fantasy of reparation and revenge as in perversion but is, rather, the result of parental attitudes, which create an all-too-conflict-free nontraumatic atmosphere in which the femininity originates. (We shall look more closely at transsexualism in chapter 8.)

This, then, is another case in which the force producing the aberrant behavior is not one of fantasy that corrects a traumatic past but more simply one of the nonpainful, nondangerous shaping of the subject's personality by dynamics constantly present in the family.

(Note: Only male transsexuals are considered here because I think the etiology in female transsexualism has more traumatic elements and is not just a variant.)

Cultural Variants

The forms that masculinity and femininity take in a culture vary from era to era (in heated-up times, from year to year) and can differ from culture to culture. It would be unwise for an observer from outside the culture (separated either by generations—even centuries—or by distance) to decide what is an aberration, much less whether what is observed is a perversion. What is aberrant between cultures may not be aberrant within a culture. In the same way, styles of erotic performance can change owing to historical and social circumstances, and one should be careful not to judge perversion (or lack of it) from a superficial glance.

A nice example—especially because it is used polemically so often these days—is the matter of homosexuality in ancient Greece. Different commentators have read the facts differently. Opinions range from the belief that this homosexuality was not a perversion because it was accepted by the whole culture to a belief that the whole culture was perverted. The version I prefer is that of Vanggaard (150). He describes the acceptable homosexuality in these Greeks as being restricted to the highest class, to men, and accepted by these men as the most honorable form of relationship. It did not displace heterosexuality. Its function was to transmit the finest ethical standards of the society. A man would bind himself to a boy, teaching him honor, strength, fidelity, and selflessness; each sexual act was an offering—in one's behavior and literally in the contribution of semen—of the precepts and the substance of manliness. Effeminacy played no part; only the man who could not do other than love men was considered homosexual in today's derogatory sense. When the young man who had been honored by his older partner's erotic behavior was well into adolescence, the relationship ended, and the young man was then expected not to persist in homosexuality —except that in time he was to treat a young man as he had been treated. The ritualized homosexuality did not displace heterosexuality but rather only the capacity equally to honor women of one's own standing.

In other words, the dynamics of this form of homosexuality were different from the standard expressed today. Hostility between the partners was not a dominant motivation (as it also occasionally is not in respecting and tender homosexual relationships today).

Vanggaard describes other cultures where similar transmission of masculinity is the main purpose of institutionalized homosexuality, which is consciously built into the culture's mystique—not the case of our culture's present-day male homosexuality (though some of these dynamics, for example, power received through incorporated semen, may be among many other dynamic forces).

This is not to say that perversion could not hide within cultural norms; if there were a custom somewhere that all men had to dress in women's clothes for a religious ceremony, there would always be a few who secretly performed the ceremony because it was sexually exciting, not because it was religiously sublime. But the rule would be the same as above: the definition of perversion would be made on the basis of what the act meant to the person.

Faute de Mieux

When, for lack of what one prefers, one settles for substitutes, the act will be aberrant but need not be perverse. Bestiality is an example. Although it is always listed as a perversion in the compendia, it may often not be so. Unless the person having intercourse with the animal does so because of a preference for animals, the motivation may not be generated by fantasy as in perversion. With sheepherders, for instance, intercourse with their flock is usually presumed to be for lack of something better, not because sheep are their favorite objects. (The only exception I know of appears in a Woody Allen movie.) If the latter is the case, look for a more complicated dynamic. In the case of the pornography in which women are seen having intercourse with animals, the chances are great that the perversion (which is not bestiality) is in the man who buys the photographs; the woman posing may be motivated by simpler needs (money) or may be a mentally defective or psychotic victim of the pornographer.

One cannot judge by an external view of the act but rather by what goes on in the performer's mind. Masturbation is an example. It is certainly normative. Its use increases when preferred objects are missing. But we

would be inaccurate to generalize that therefore masturbation is not perverse. Most often, even when masturbation is *faute de mieux,* the pornography used (either public
pornography or private pornography, that is, daydreams) will have perverse elements. In this situation,
the fantasy is used because it satisfies what cannot be
satisfied in an actual sex act with another. In that case,
masturbation is not just a substitute but a truly distinctive sexual act with its own specific motives and energies.
So also with the use of prostitutes. A man may have to
turn to prostitutes because he cannot do better: he is a
Yukon gold miner and the only available women are
whores. But what if he is a stockbroker in New York who
is impotent except with an officially degraded woman?

The issue of *faute de mieux,* therefore, is not always
clear-cut. Often, even under circumstances of deprivation, the fantasy used reveals the act to be a mixture of
the lack of something better plus the opportunity for
using perverse fantasy, in daydream or pornography.

The Animal Argument:
An Alleged Category

In asking that we talk of variants or deviations rather
than perversions, sex experts today, allied with others
fighting for sexual civil rights, use observations of animal
behavior. As was seen in chapter 2, the argument goes
that although one finds innumerable examples of sexual
aberrance in them, animals cannot be accused of willful,
obstinate, wicked behavior. Humans are linked to other
animals by similar brain structures, physiological mechanisms, and behavior. Therefore perversion does not
exist in us, for the roots for aberration are phylogenetic.
But when one makes a male rat attempt intercourse with
a male cat by giving the rat a substance that damages
brain function, it is not proved either that rats as a species have an unconscious desire to rape cats or that, at

an earlier stage in evolution, rats' ancestors were either homosexual or susceptible to bestiality (desire for cats).

Nonetheless, I agree with those who call these behaviors in animals variants. But I disagree with them on the larger issue; the error in logic comes only if one says that because animals are not perverse, because there are brain structures available to start and guide all sorts of behavior, because animals can be forced by experimentally driving the brain with hormones, drugs, electricity, or surgery, or because animals can be experimentally conditioned, then these same stimuli, because they are at times at work in humans, are *the* causes of our species' aberrance. That is poor argument.

Perversion is exclusively human.

Chapter 4

Perversions: Aberrations That Are Not Variants

Chapter 2 reviewed arguments sex researchers use to deny that aberrance can be due to willed—moral—choice. Let us extend that discussion, leaving behind the study of animals, of the brain, of evolution, of statistics, of samples—all important but dangerous to linger over here. From now on, I shall emphasize an element—known but not directly observable—that challenges that research: *desire* as a primary motivation for behavior. To the physiologist, the awareness "I want" may be a mirage, just an emanation of the brain; to the strict behaviorist, it is a manifestation, a correlate, or a result, but not a cause; to the statistician, it is a superfluous effect in a world whose inevitability is predetermined by that prime mover, the bell curve: without the urge of "I want," actions and drives would still supposedly distribute themselves from likely to unlikely. But there is no question that we who feel these attitudes are simplistic are not home free when we recognize that desire is a true cause of behavior; no one has learned to handle desire in the laboratory. Even when language is available for expressing feelings, we cannot accurately measure something as complex, paradoxical, variable, and contradictory as our desire for, rage against, envy of, pleasure in, or love of another person. How much less, then, can we know the mind—or more accurately, the protomind—of the preverbal infant, one of the necessary objects of a study of perversion. Well-bred scientists, deprived of all but fragments of the experimental method in the face of mental life, shun study of the effect of desire on sexual function and especially of the origins of desire in the whirlwinds of infancy. At the extreme, some even deny that desire exists.

The additional evidence, I repeat, that shifts our opinion from the conclusion of modern sex researchers that humans do not choose their sexual styles but have behavior thrust on them is found in the study of *fantasy,* that vehicle of hope, healer of trauma, protector from reality, concealer of truth, fixer of identity, restorer of tranquillity, enemy of fear and sadness, cleanser of the soul. And creator of perversion. Since Freud first showed it, we have known that in humans fantasy is as much part of the etiology of perversions—more, of all sexual excitement —as are the physiological and environmental factors the sex researchers are helping us understand. The details of the perversion—the story line—are incomprehensible in their origin and meaning if one ignores the process and function of fantasy. You can study every cell of the brain and every animal in the kingdom and not know why a man gets excited by wearing a woman's shoe, or by a dead body, or by an amputee, or by a child, or by a penis. Even more, if one examines the fantasy, ignoring no details, I think one finds embedded therein remnants of the individual's experiences with other people who in the real world, during childhood, provoked the reaction that we call perversion. And at the center is hostility.

When we expand our definition by using hostility as the measure, we now include a lot of sexual behavior, certainly much that is ubiquitous and therefore, in a statistical sense, not even an aberrance. The hostility is often easy to find. For a number of perversions, it is a central feature of the manifest content and marks, even for the untrained observer, the bizarreness of the condition. The more gross the hostility, the less question that one is dealing with perversion. Murder that sexually excites, mutilation for excitement, rape, sadism with precise physical punishments such as whipping or cutting, enchaining and binding games, defecating or urinating on one's object—all are on a lessening scale of conscious rage toward one's sex object, in which an essential purpose is for one to be superior to, harmful to, triumphant over another. And so it is also in the nonphysical sadisms like exhibitionism, voyeurism, dirty phone calls or letters, use of prostitutes, and most forms of promiscuity. Statistics, watching animals, and manipulating the brain put us nowhere in understanding why and how these excitements work, but getting into another's mind and searching out the nature and origin of the need to harm one's partner are possible and tell a great deal.

Take the most common of these behaviors, promiscuity, the one with the least hostility visible, the one most often used these days for discussion by those who would free up society by arguing that if a behavior is ubiquitous it is normal. The logic goes like this:

1. Most animals are not monogamous; man is an animal.

2. Promiscuous desires are found in almost all humans and therefore are far from statistically aberrant.

3. Those who deny having such desires and those unable to act on them are not superior and sinless, as they claim, but cramped and inhibited; the ideals of the Victorian era have been unmasked.

4. Therefore, let people enjoy their bodies freely if they wish, so long as they do not victimize others.

5. When that is done, it will be seen that the term "perversion" was only one more technique a frightened, inhibited society used to protect its massive neurosis.

I almost completely agree with the argument. As technique for social action it is quite good, for it is, I believe, almost correct, a good mix of observations and sensible conclusions. It lets us conclude that promiscuity is fun, harmless, invigorating, mind-expanding, and liberating for society. But can one thus short-cut his personal—albeit neurotic—sense of sin? The error is that the argument leaves out the hostility. Think of the Don Juan, that paradigm of promiscuity, who reveals his hatred of women so innocently and unwittingly to the audience he must gather to vouch for his performance: his interests are in seduction, not love, and in recounting for friends how many women he has had and how they degraded themselves in the needfulness of the passion he induced. His excitement and gratification do not come from the sensual pleasures of the sexual act or the intimacy that he might have established with another person; in fact, he shows little interest in intercourse, his concentration being on overcoming the resistance of an apparently reluctant woman. Easy women do not attract him. His unending, frantic need to prove himself—his gratification only in numbers of conquests—reveals that his body is more in the service of power than of erotism.

So, we ought not to generalize, when we see a promiscuous person, that he is simply a free soul, expressing the natural sexual exuberance inherent in the species as we all would were we not enslaved by society. Such could be the case, and perhaps will be in time if society shifts, but it is the difference in what the act means to us that measures whether it is perverse or not, not what anatomical parts are used on whom or what. (Nonhostile, joyous promiscuity is portrayed regularly in books, films, and the theater, creating the illusion that it is not rare.)

Then there are sexual styles in which the actor seems the victim, rather than the perpetrator, of hostility: those who hang or anesthetize themselves to have an orgasm, those who need to be bound in ropes, chains, or tight garments, those who wish to be beaten or cut, those who are excited when defecated or urinated on, those who endlessly choose partners who humiliate and abandon them. Here, hostility in the perverted act is disguised, maintained secretly in the fantasies of what one is doing to one's partner when one is "victimized." These people have lusciously martyrish gratifications, such as "they'll-be-sorry-when-I'm-gone" or "at-least-God-loves-me" or "contrast-my-saintliness-with-those-who-hurt-me," which convert the physical victim into psychological victor over his tormentor; the act is performed before a fantasied audience whose function is to recognize that the sadistic partner is a brute. In addition, as creator of the performance, the masochist is never truly a victim, because he never really relinquishes control, and in that sense the whole scenario is known (preconsciously if not consciously) to portray only fraudulent suffering. I doubt if masochists, in the strict sense of sexual perversion, often choose sadists, in the strict sense of sexual perversion, for their sexual partners. I would think that each intuitively knows, when observing the other's excitement, that the partner's fantasies do not fit his. If a sadist's partner is lustful, then the sadist knows the partner is not the humiliated sufferer fantasy demands, no matter how many welts are raised or how many painful cries elicited. This is an example of the masochistic contract Smirnoff has described (129).

Freud long ago (24) noted that sadism and masochism are partners. And countless people, from analysts with their patients to spouses of the masochists, have been the focus of the sadism (retribution and restitution) in masochism. A patient says with quiet sadness, apologetically, and with understanding of my great goodness, "I don't blame you that you can't stand my sweat on your couch" (which, being leather, bears the proof of her suffering). Of course, what she is saying is, "You beast; you allege you're an analyst—a physician, healer, empathizer, understander, and forgiver of the natural pain of humanity —but actually you cannot escape your past: you are a *male* and are disgusted with my female body's dirty secretions." Her sexual fantasy, from adolescence till her masochism was analyzed, was that a frozen-cold, sadistic male director forced her to be raped into a frenzy of excitement by a sexually crazed stallion in a public performance on a stage witnessed by a circle of silent men with erections.

Finally, there are the perversions in which hostility of any sort seems absent—the fetishisms. These range from necrophilia (where one chooses a corpse one has not oneself killed) through the use of inanimate objects (usually garments whose connection with a human object has been reduced to the symbolic) to the ubiquitous fetishism of treating people as if they were only organs (for example, breasts or penis) or functions (beater, screwer, victim, automaton, slave). Since hostility often seems absent, especially in the classic fetishisms, which use inanimate objects such as garments, these ought to test the hypothesis of hostility's presence more vigorously than do the sadistic and masochistic perversions, where the hostility is so patently visible.

A closer view of fetishism shows that the desire to harm is only silent, hidden. When one challenges, "Where is the hostility in becoming excited by a piece of cloth?" an answer is possible. In the next chapter, we shall look at that great dehumanizing device—pornography—and examine a case that makes explicit my proposition about hostility. This patient shows us the anger hidden in the fetish and, beyond that (as I believe is true for all perversion), the source of the anger in the patient's victimization in childhood, usually by parents or their surrogates. Through the perversion, anger is transformed into a victory over those who made him wretched, for in perversion, trauma becomes triumph.

Part II

Dynamics: Trauma, Hostility, Risk, and Revenge

Chapter 5

Pornography
and Perversion

If fantasy is what determines whether or not any given sexual act is perverse, then we should look more closely at what an individual is thinking and feeling in order to understand his perversion. Pornography allows us to do this with ease.

Pornography is a complex daydream in which activities, usually but not necessarily overtly sexual, are projected into written, pictorial, or aural material to induce genital excitement in an observer. No depiction is pornographic until an observer's fantasies are added; nothing is pornographic per se.

Here is the cover picture from a pornographic pamphlet, that is, a booklet produced by someone who thought there was a large enough audience to make the printing profitable. The booklet was purchased by a man who knew it would excite him sexually. Those who look at this picture can be divided into those who get excited and those who do not. The latter group, I assume, is by far the larger. Most readers will be unable to understand why the picture and its story excite; they will not even seriously believe the pamphlet could do so.

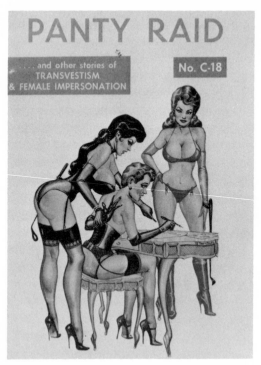

What—if you are not a transvestite—do you see in the picture? Probably not very much: just women who are supposed to depict powerful, dangerous, feminine beauty and who are bullying a defenseless, cowering, humiliated man dressed in women's garments.

Each of the many genres of pornography is created for a specific perverse need by exact attention to detail, and each defines an area of excitement that will have no effect on a different person. Thus, for example, a sadist will choose depictions of sadistic acts, and a fetishistic transvestite will choose depictions of acts of cross-dressing. As with all perversions, pornography is a matter of aesthetics: one man's delight is another's boredom. Also, as with all perversions, at its heart is a fantasied act of revenge, condensing in itself the subject's sexual life history—his memories and fantasies, traumas, frustrations, and joys. There is always a victim, no matter how disguised: no victim, no pornography. The use of such matter is an act of perversion with several components. The most apparent is voyeurism. The second, hidden (unless the person is an overt sexual sadist), is sadism; sadism is, however, rather easily demonstrated. The third, more hidden (unless the person is an overt sexual masochist), is masochism; masochism is hard to demonstrate, since it is hidden in an unconscious identification with the depicted victim.

These three components are universal for users of pornography. To be dwelled on more in this chapter is a fourth component, which is specific to each user—his own style of perversion.

Pornography is for restitution; its creation and its use are ritualized acts, and deviation from a narrow, prescribed path will produce decreased sexual excitement. The perversion functions as a necessary preserver of potency. The actual sexual life history—the unconscious memory of real historical events—exists in the conscious fantasies expressed in the pornography.

The development of the manifest complex daydream that the pornography exteriorizes is a chronicle, over the years, of fantasies, each elaboration occurring at the moment when a piece of pain (or of incomplete pleasure) is converted into (greater) pleasure, until all these fantasies, like building blocks, have been assembled to create the adult perversion that presents itself overtly. But there is a grain of historical reality embedded in each fantasy, and the differences between what actually happened in different people's lives account in good part (though not completely) for the minor variations found even in a group of people homogeneous for a particular perversion.

Let us examine pornography of the perversion

transvestism* (fetishistic cross-dressing) to find these
bits of historical reality. There should be an advantage
for us in using such an odd condition for our example,
for it is pretty rare and its pornography does not stir
anyone but a transvestite. (One might suggest, not quite
seriously, that a test to establish the diagnosis of transvestism or any perversion in men would be to show its
pornography to several subjects: only those with increased penile blood flow would fit the diagnosis. One
cannot ask for a more rapid, precise diagnostic procedure. Such a test would also demonstrate most concretely that the psychodynamics of transvestites are
different from those of other people.)

In the pornographic literature catering to transvestites, there are repeated stories with the same theme—
a frightened, pathetic, defenseless boy-man finds himself, through no doing of his own, trapped by powerful,
dangerously beautiful women, who bully and humiliate
him. The poor victim—the peak of whose victimization
is illustrated by the women physically forcing him to put
on women's clothes—hardly seems a subject created for
inducing sexual excitement. Yet the men who need such
material find their greatest anticipation just at this point
in the story, when the humiliated man is illustrated being
exposed to his greatest anguish. The typical picture and
accompanying text show him seated, cowering, while
standing over him with threatening gestures and looks
are the very phallic women. (The term "phallic" here is
not simply the application of a concept: the drawings
show repeated themes of phallic-shaped objects—sti-
letto heels, table and chair legs, whips, pens.)

Here are excerpts from the pornography. Fraternity
pledge Bruce King, as part of his initiation, has to raid
the clothesline of a sorority house, when "squeals and

*I shall use the term "transvestism" only for those in whom clothes
of the opposite sex cause erotic excitement. There are other conditions in which cross-dressing occurs (139), but they are different from
fetishistic cross-dressing and need not be confused with it.

bubbling laughter" suddenly envelop him. He is caught
and bound by sorority girls, all of them "shrieking with
joy."

> He tried to protest but his gag was too tight; he wiggled
> but only succeeded in getting the brunt of their sharp
> fingernails into the muscular flesh of his flanks and
> thighs. This brought much raucous laughter from the
> victorious vixens who thrilled at the helpless struggles of
> their male captive. . . .
>   The girl named Lori, apparently the group leader, was
> a silver-blonde Amazon. She must have stood a statu-
> esque six feet tall, proudly erect, her heaving bosom
> thrust forth with a strange form of arrogance which de-
> manded obedience and respect. Lori was garbed in a
> tight fitting buckled beauty of a pure satin dress; it fea-
> tured a permanently pleated skirt which shivered like so
> many leather strings with each movement. The turquoise
> blouse boasted floral and fruit decorations. Lori's waist
> was captivated [*sic*] by a huge patent leather belt of shin-
> ing black; the contrasting silver buckle resembled a lock,
> with a tiny keyhole which defied entrance and exit. Her
> hips were forced into a figure-training position so that
> she walked with some difficulty, but with greater pride.
> And Lori's shoes: they were the heavenly dream of any
> clothes raider. The unbelievably thin match-stick high
> heels must have been a perfect seven inches long! Made
> of shiny white patent leather—believe it or not—the shoe
> featured a slinky sling back which was a silvery chain, a
> *peau de sole* [*sic*] trim, an open toe through which peeped
> a gleaming red nail, the toe almost grateful to be liber-
> ated from its confinement. The vamp was charmingly
> decorated with a pair of gleaming glass eyes! Yes, the
> eyes even winked wickedly as Lori moved her slender
> legs. Such white patent leather, polished to milky perfec-
> tion, deserved respect as they were held in awe and es-
> teem! As Lori stamped her dainty but powerfully shod
> foot, tiny sparks escaped from the stiletto 7 inch heel!
>   Bruce flinched, struggling against the bonds of the
> robe belts. "Lori," his voice tried to be fierce and confi-
> dent, "will you cut me loose? All right, so I didn't suc-

ceed in my panty raid. I lost! The frat brothers will give me a real paddling," he squirmed at the thought, "and that'll be that. So let's just forget it."

"Oh, we don't want you to be paddled out of your fraternity, no sir!" another girl said. "Lori, what say we give him . . . what's your name . . ."

"Bruce . . . Bruce King."

". . . let's give Bruce a complete feminine outfit to bring back to his frat brothers. This will be something he shall long remember!" Lori smiled. As she folded both of her slender swan-like arms across her chest, Bruce caught sight of her blood-red fingernails, extended like the talons of a wicked vulture! "Very well, Sandra. We'll give Bruce a nice frilly outfit . . . bloomers, slip, bra, dress, silk stockings which attach to the garter straps of the garter belt we'll also let him have, and a nice pair of high-heeled shoes . . ."

Before Bruce could protest, he found himself descended upon by the girls, who ripped off his simple white business shirt, cotton khaki trousers (he was grateful he wore protective boxer shorts), off went his moccasins, wool socks. "It's cold . . ." he shivered, feeling more embarrassed and humiliated than the elements of the weather in early spring. To be stripped, bound and in the captivity of four domineering types of females was certainly an experience that shattered his manhood. There was no telling what they could do to make good a threat that Lori now voiced: "We'll teach him that the female of the species are the *real* aggressive members of the human race! . . ."

"We're going to dress you, Bruce," purred Lori, her green eyes glittering with a strange fascination of the spectacle of a man being held in her captivity. "Now, girls —get those boxer shorts of his and throw them out . . . good boys shouldn't wear such sloppy things. We'll teach our Brucie how to dress."

"No! No!" he protested, but four sets of female hands yanked down his boxer shorts. With a sigh of relief, he remembered he wore his tiny athletic supporter which the girls ridiculed by giggling, "Look—he wears a G-string!"

Lori then said, "Okay, girls, untie him. It'll be easier to get his clothes on. But Brucie-boy," she said in a falsetto tone, "you won't get very far—in your G-string. So behave yourself, or we'll take that away from you, too."

Bruce flushed and no sooner were his arms and legs freed than he tried to cover himself with his hands but his awkward knock-kneed position and round shouldered position of embarrassment only provoked more laughter. "Very funny! Very funny!" he gasped. "Come on, girls," laughed Lori. "I can hardly wait to see what he looks like in some really dainty clothes. Let's start with this panty . . ."

Lori held up a few brassieres and finally made her selection of a charming item. "See, Bruce," she dangled it before him, as if threatening his manhood, "this brassiere has in-up pushup pads and foam rubber shapemakers. This low plunge front gives real cleavage; to a girl, it's breathtakingly sinful. To you," and she made a throaty laugh, "it'll be very wicked . . ."

He would make no protest. It would only infuriate the girls and they might intensify their hatred upon him. And now . . . yes . . . here it was: the gown to be worn by Bruce King.

"Do you like it?" asked Lori, already joining in giggling with the other girls at the anticipation of seeing him wear a dress. "It's a French import. It's an exclusive design." The color was Vampire Red! The gown featured a gossamer silk sheer V-insert lined in nude, exciting "nail-heads" and a braid trim. The back was plunging. The sleeves were made of transparent net-like soft silk of smoke-red. The waist was captured with a very tight suede belt, its buckle a huge replica of Satan, with twin fangs for an insert. A tiny Devil's pitchfork pointed at the buckle which was polished silver. The skirt of this unusual gown was scintillating in its 3 rows of 6″ fringes made of leather. Each fringe was as delicate as a shoe lace but as strong as the reins used to compel a team of horses to do the bidding of the driver. With each movement of the hips, the 3 rows of fringes would dance in all directions, as would a group of frenzied primitive worshippers before a weird fetish-God.

As the dress was lowered upon Bruce, he found his heart was pounding, his emotions were stepped up and he was breathless with eager anticipation. He dared not admit his true feelings to anyone; even to himself! After all, he had been FORCED into this whole thing . . . by his frat brothers and then he was CAPTURED and BOUND BY FEMALES and compelled to follow their orders . . .

How can humiliation produced on being forced to put on women's clothes by hostile women cause sexual excitement? There are several explanations that can (almost) account for this excitement.*

First, although the man in the illustration is humiliated, the man reading the book is humiliated only in effigy; while he identifies with the illustrated man, he is very clearly also safely not so identified. He knows this experience, taking place via pornography, is only a fantasy.

Second, the excitement is accompanied by a guilt-removing device inherent in the story: since the pathetic boy-man is being forced to dress by the cruel women, he cannot be accused of wanting to do this himself. (In pornography, as in humor, there is always a device for reducing guilt. This could be true for many other sublimated activities with hostile components, such as the theater, visual arts, and "normal" sexual relations . . . Imagine considering heterosexual intercourse a "sublimated activity"!)

*We do not quite know how sexual excitement is produced in anyone, not just in the perverse. How does a woman ('s body) excite a heterosexual man? What has he learned from infancy on and how do the nongenital responses of infancy and childhood become converted into the adult genital response? Is the explanation simply physiological? (Not likely.) Does anxiety play a role in normal persons as in the perverse? Just as Masters and Johnson did the naturalist's task of revealing the gross physical appearance of sexual excitement, so should the mechanisms of the psychological experience of sexual excitement be discovered—what sets it off, what maintains and protects it, what makes it recur or subside in time into boredom.

Yet the two reasons above are only secondary devices to *protect* the excitement and are not causes in themselves. We come closer if we study the life history that is present in the pornography in such condensed fashion.

The man who first showed me these dynamics, who also brought in the pamphlet just quoted, had been forced to dress thus by women in childhood. I have told his story before (137, 142).

Fortunately for the research (and disastrously for him), he was posed for snapshots, placed quite openly in the family album, tracing the development of his cross-dressing. In addition, the women who did it to him are alive; though I could not interview them, they gave information to him and his wife, filling in the story indicated by the snapshots.

The patient is a biologically normal man in his mid-thirties, married and with children. The dominating interest in his life is sexual excitement produced by women's clothes; he is masculine in behavior, in choice of clothes when not expressing his perversion, and in profession.

For the first almost three years of his life, he was treated by his mother and father as if he were what he was, a normal male whom they expected to grow up to be a man. They gave him an unequivocally masculine name at birth and sent out no covert messages to contradict their recognition that his assignment to the male sex was correct. As a result, he developed, as do almost all little boys, the conviction that he belonged to the male sex, a necessary first stage in the development of masculinity in all males. Then his mother developed a chronic illness that removed her from the home, ending with her death less than two years later. When she was first hospitalized, his father mobilized the boy's aunt and this aunt's teen-age daughter to take care of the child. These two women unfortunately shared an immense hatred for males and for males' masculinity. Given the freedom to act upon him, they were able safely to attack his expanding masculinity. They did so by altering his appearance. It is easy; women can simply put unmasculine or even women's clothes on a boy. What incites them to do this, I underline, is his already present masculinity; that is what they hate, and it is best attacked, they know, by damaging, not destroying it. Such women do not want the boy not to be a male; rather, they want to assuage their envy by saying that maleness is unimportant and inferior. To do so, they make clear to themselves and to the boy that they wish to humiliate him, which requires that he forever retain his wish to be a male and his awareness that he can be humiliated.

On his fourth birthday, a few weeks before she died, his mother came home to visit him. On that occasion, the aunt and cousin introduced his mother to "a new neighbor girl," in fact the dying woman's son, and took photographs to memorialize the joke. The man who had been this boy has no memory of that traumatic event; it was only discovered by his wife in a family album, during the time they were being seen by me. The story was then corroborated by the aunt.

So far as we know, sexual excitement began two or three years later. Only at this point does the patient's memory regarding transvestism begin. At that time, as a punishment, he was forced by another woman to put on her stockings. He was instantly struck by a voluptuous feeling he is sure he had never experienced before. As pleasurable as it was, he also sensed an aura of guilt and so for several years repeated the experience only a few times. At puberty, however, it became linked to orgasm and from then to now it has been his dominating pleasure. Even during intercourse, he is fully potent only when cross-dressed. (Perhaps not coincidentally, the woman who cross-dressed him as punishment had a son who was treated similarly; I have a picture of him, dressed as Shirley Temple.)

Throughout those years of childhood and then on into

adolescence and adulthood to the present, his masculinity was not destroyed, only damaged. That is how
the attacking women would have wished it; had he
turned completely into a normal-appearing "woman,"
they would have lost their victim. But instead, he struggled secretly against them so as to protect this essence
of his self.

I have discussed elsewhere (137) the evidence that the
core of one's gender identity—the sense of being a male
or a female—is laid down by the first three years of life
and is pretty much unalterable thereafter, as was true
with this boy. If one has developed that sense unequivocally, later experiences can threaten it, forcing modifications upon one as one attempts to protect that core, but
the core will remain.

Up to now, we have noted the effort the traumatized
child makes to save himself. The case above exemplifies
this struggle but also, by introducing the issue of threat
to one's masculinity or femininity, expands our understanding of the precise nature of that victimhood: the
fear that one's already established sense of belonging to
one's sex may be destroyed. In analytic circles, this is
called "castration anxiety";* but that term is too narrow,
for one fears more than the loss of one's genitals. Rather,
it is that if one loses one's genitals, that may signify a
more profound loss, one's no longer belonging to the
class male, the conviction of which is at the core of one's
being. Adult males whose genitals are damaged or destroyed do not lose their sense of maleness, much less
their sense of existing; while the experience is traumatic,
it does not create perversion or—in the person with intact gender identity—psychosis.

I would disagree with the behavioristic explanation,

---

*Fenichel summarizes in classical language: "The pervert is a per-
son whose sexual pleasure is blocked by the idea of castration.
Through the perversion he tries to prove that there is no castration.
In so far as this proof is believed, sexual pleasure and orgasm become
possible again" (18, p. 327).

however, that the perverse act is only fortuitously linked
—conditioned—to the daydream or the enactment of the
daydream (in the transvestite, for instance, when he puts
on women's clothes for the first time). The behavioristic
explanation attempts to remove one's childhood and
psychodynamics; it seems to say that *any* object or event
occurring at the first time of maximum pleasure would
be the beginning of that form of sexual excitement. Analysts, on the contrary, believe that that is an end point
and that the agent of the excitement, for example,
women's clothes, was not fortuitous but suitable, anticipated, and even chosen. Taking a careful history will
confirm this analytic position.

To return to our case, the patient was able to maintain
a sense of maleness and masculinity over the years despite the threat produced by his tormentors. Transvestites are long since known—as was this man—to be
masculine-appearing men except when sexually excited.
They are not, as are effeminate homosexuals, habitually
caricaturing women. Almost always, they are overtly
heterosexual, usually married and with children, and
able to carry themselves in a masculine way without
effort.

But where, in our patient, are the hostility, revenge,
and triumph anticipated in my earlier remarks? If the
thesis is correct, they will appear in the transvestite's
sexual fantasy. We assume that, when forced into an
unmasculine role by being cross-dressed, the boy felt
threatened to his depths, and we expect him to have tried
to protect himself as all children do, by creating a com-
forting daydream. We know of that daydream, because
transvestites tell it, react to it when it is told to them in
their pornography, and act it out when dressed up. Let
us study it again.

Each historical event now to be recounted appears in
the pornography.

History. From birth to age three, the boy developed in a masculine manner.

Pornography. The story starts with a masculine heterosexual man, who has shown no fetishistic interest before in women's clothes or any feminine or effeminate mannerisms.

History. When the boy was three, his mother left the family and his "mothering" was turned over to an aunt and older cousin, both of whom despised males. *Concurrently*

Pornography. The man is trapped by a group of females, who make fun of his maleness and immediately overpower him.

History. His father was almost never home day or night, for years, and in effect abandoned the boy to the women.

Pornography. There is no other man in the story.

History. These two women designed and fashioned new clothes, ruffled and effeminate-looking, for the little boy. Later they dressed him, not just effeminately, but in girls' clothes "as a joke."

Pornography. The dangerous women force the man, who is filled with shame and humiliation, to put on women's clothes. Yet they are portrayed as joking and laughing.

History. The women, being older and bigger, were psychologically immensely powerful and physically overpowered him without a struggle.

Pornography. The man does not have the strength to struggle, much less escape.

History. Nevertheless, the little boy needed and wanted, even loved, these women. What choice did he have at three, or four, or five years? They served not only as models for identification but as desired heterosexual objects, for they were now his "mother."

Pornography. The women are drawn as phallic and dangerous but also beautiful and feminine.

History. Despite dressing him on occasion in girls' clothes, these women always left him the knowledge he was male and had masculinity. Except for the rare occasions when he was cross-dressed, he wore masculine clothes. His games and hobbies have always been masculine. He is now a leader of men in a masculine business. To make their own satisfaction exquisite, they had to prove that masculinity was worthless, far beneath their desire. To accomplish this, they had to be sure not to destroy it, only make it foolish. So he was not feminized to the degree that he wished his body changed to a female one or lost the pleasure of his penis.

Pornography. The man is clearly identified as a male; this is never denied. His name is strongly masculine and is not changed by the women during the story. The women express recognition that he is masculine. The attack is specifically aimed, not at damaging his maleness, but at his identity, his masculine attributes, of which the most visible are clothes. In transvestite pornography a male is not turned into a female.

History. The disaster became a triumph. By age six, he was sexually excited putting on a woman's garment.

Pornography. After the trauma, the man senses in himself an intense, growing sensualness for the women's clothes that had at first been forced on him.

History. His fetishistic cross-dressing gradually increased in frequency and completeness to dressing quite like a woman, so that added to it was a nongenitally exciting pleasure in being fully dressed as a woman.

Pornography. The man, near the end of the story, is dressed completely as a woman.

History. He found an apparently benign, gentle woman, who married him although knowing of (in fact, I learned after a few years, because of) his transvestism. She enjoyed helping him buy women's clothes and wigs and taught him to dress stylishly, apply make-up properly, and carry himself like a woman. (This type of woman and her relationship to transvestism is discussed elsewhere [137].)

Pornography. The harpies are now gentle, friendly, and accepting, fully feminine, and rather girlish.

History. He presently goes into the world, passing intermittently as a woman.

Pornography. All leave together, the man looking like a normal woman; he is promised that they will all do it again soon, next time as friends.

All that is missing in the pornography, but which occurs in transvestites, is a latency period after the trauma, a matter of months or years during which there is no evidence of overt transvestism, following which the first surface manifestation of the perversion appears (that is, sexual excitement produced by women's clothes). This latency period, being silent, has never been studied. One can therefore only surmise that during it the boy is developing a system of fantasies to preserve his masculinity against the onslaught upon his identity by the hating female who, *in reality,* jeopardized his sense of maleness and masculinity.

It is not coincidental that he creates his success exactly at the point of disaster. That is, he uses agents of the trauma—women's clothes and the appearance of femininity—to preserve his masculinity and potency. This is not to say that this is all that is needed to create the perversion, for, while the fear of being unmanned is crucial, so also is the (defensive) construction that the powerful women have penises and the power of supermen (18, 32, 35). As noted, this too is indicated in the pornography.

I have tried to detail—here and elsewhere (137, 147) —the nature of this specific trauma (attempted feminization by older, powerful females) by reporting case material showing the contributions made by mothers (and their substitutes) and fathers in helping create a transvestite. These data suggest that *in fetishistic cross-dressing the denied threat of castration and the phallic women imagined are based on historical reality.* In these patients, it really did happen that the boy was threatened with loss of masculinity and humiliated by females more powerful than he, not just in some general way, but very precisely by being put into women's clothes. (Although without evidence to prove it, I suspect that the cross-dressing of a little boy is deeply traumatic only if he was already damaged in the years of development before the first overt humiliation. There must also be little boys who, after being cross-dressed by a girl or woman, simply are not susceptible enough to that sort of victimization to take it seriously.)

Just where are we to find the supposed triumph that preserves the transvestite's potency? It cannot come simply from reliving a trauma. How, if the trauma is recapitulated in the perversion, does pleasure replace anguish? I presume, as with other episodes of mastery, that it comes from such sources as finding that one has actually, over and over, survived the trauma, or from the infinite uses to which repression and denial can be put. More specifically, however, the following are suggested: (1) Conversion of a sense of being damaged and inferior into exhibitionistic fantasies ("See what a lovely woman I make"). (2) "Self-realization," the gradual self-conscious creation of a fully evolved "feminine" role: some transvestites learn to act so much like women that they can pass as such undetected publicly.

More important: (3) Fantasies (conscious, preconscious, and unconscious) of revenge against women, which create an exultant sense of redressing the balance. (4) Identifying in the pornography and other fantasy life not only with the humiliated male but with the masterful aggressor, the phallic woman.

The victim becomes victor. The little boy was humbled, but there—now—presides the adult pervert, dressed in the women's clothes. These garments, formerly the agent of trauma, now delight him—strong, full of anticipation, powerfully potent, intact, penis and self gathered up in full strength, competent for orgasm. How better to prove he is triumphant than to be potent in the presence of the original trauma? He has his revenge. The women, so mysteriously powerful in childhood, while not reduced in strength, are not able to overpower him; he proves it every time he puts on their clothes. On each occasion his penis demonstrates that they have failed: he has successfully defended himself and thus frustrated them.

But unfortunately, he has to repeat endlessly, for somehow he knows the perversion is only a construction, a fantasy; it can never truly prove that he has won. It does so only for the moment, and each time in his life that circumstances arise to echo the original traumatic situation, he can placate his anxiety only in repeating the perverse act whose function is to tell him again that he is intact and a victor.

An essential quality in pornography (and perversion) is sadism—revenge for a passively experienced trauma. I am not only referring to well-known revenge fantasies and sexual acts found also in nontransvestite men, such as those of poisoning or humiliating one's partner with ejaculate or of physical damage to someone by one's phallic onslaught. I suppose these are at times present in transvestites, but, additionally and more important, the transvestite revenges himself just by being able to get an erection. That is, he succeeds with a woman when he was supposed to have failed. Even more triumphantly, he succeeds at exactly that moment that should be the moment of greatest failure, when he is dressed as a woman and should be humiliated. Of course, one crucial fact sustains him when he is so dressed: his constant awareness that he has a penis under the woman's clothes, which makes him, too, a phallic woman. Freud and most analysts since believe the fantasy of a woman with a phallus is always an invention a boy (man) finds necessary to deny that the awfulness that is castration could happen to him. In this theory, females are fundamentally—anatomically—inferior unless given a prosthesis. I think this is not always or only the case. When men in fantasy give women a phallus, they may do so to deny not women's inferiority but female superiority; it replaces for males a fear of the mystery of female generative capacity—inner hidden power, as in procreation or life-and-death omnipotence over their infant—with the familiar, a penis. Later (chaps. 6 and 8) we shall return to this subject.

In the pornography, the moment of greatest anticipation of pleasure—the come-on illustration on the cover of the booklet—is just when the story describes how the victim is told by the powerful women that he must put on or has just been placed in women's clothes. It is no coincidence, therefore, that the fantasy picks out the moment of greatest trauma for what is now its moment of greatest thrill. There is no more perfect triumph than to succeed after running the precise risks that had undone one in childhood. (There are similarities between this and other counterphobic triumphs, such as automobile racing, stage acting, parachute jumping, competition in sports, and so many other acutely anxiety-provoking situations of potential victory.)

Who is the victim in this transvestite fantasy? In the manifest daydream, it is the pictured transvestite-in-the-making with whom the observing transvestite consciously identifies. But additionally and unconsciously the victim is the pictured cruel phallic woman, for the transvestite, in the reality of his masturbation, is having the final victory over such a woman. Despite all she did to him in his childhood to ruin his masculinity, he has escaped her—though barely, and at the price of a severely compromised potency that can succeed only by means of perversion.

Yet he does win; he has survived. His penis is not only preserved; now, as he celebrates his sacrament, he feels himself no longer split but concentratedly unified in his sexual excitement.

He identifies with the aggressor and then (as may often be the case with the use of this mechanism) he believes (tries to believe) he is better than the aggressor: a better woman than any woman, for he possesses the best of both sexes. He is always aware of his masculinity (an essential part of transvestism), and he is aware of his femininity. He feels that, having been a man and living intermittently as a man, he has a keen eye for what is most to be appreciated in women, and being a "woman" permits him to put this into action. At a deeper level, he believes himself (is constantly working to make himself believe he is) a better woman than any woman because he is the only woman who surely has a penis. And now, identified with the powerful women, he is no longer the humiliated little boy; he no longer consciously experiences that part of him during the act of perversion. It exists overtly only in the script. He has found a way to be the sadist, expressing that satisfaction by saying he is not the depicted frightened boy-man of the story. In splitting his identification into victim and victor, he is able to satisfy, as it were, two different people inside himself.

Yet transvestites are, in the great majority, overtly heterosexual and yearn for heterosexuality, having to work against an unconscious pull toward identification with women. Considering intimacy with a living woman to be desirable but dangerous, they substitute her inert clothes for her living skin. Note these descriptions of women's clothes taken from the booklet: "The straps were milky-way white; the sheer fabric was bewitching"; "pure silk"; "pure satin"; "panties virginal white in color"; "skin tight"; "transparent green, like sea foam"; "cool, silky-soft, sensuously intimate"; "filmy"; "smoothly formed"; "blushing pink"; "delicately molded"; "transparent net-like soft silk," and so forth for many pages.

The experience is bisexual: not only is the transvestite making contact fetishistically (safely, indirectly) with women's skin (taking the woman as a heterosexual object), but he is also putting it on (identifying with the woman).

This description leaves out much that is important—and speculative—such as a fuller investigation of the transvestite's belief in phallic women, both the powerful sort who originally attacked him and the kind that he represents with his erect penis beneath the women's clothes; or the symbolic meanings the clothes have for him (for example, intact penis); or castration anxiety; or the garments as transitional objects between his mother and separation from her; and a host of additional psychoanalytic formulations. They will not be detailed here, as the present task is simply to define the concept of perversion.*

*There are too many explanations. Psychoanalytic theory is the most syncretic system since the Roman pantheon; a new Logos may be added on without displacing any of the older elements: the garments of the other sex allegedly also symbolize father's penis; or getting into mother's skin and thus being sheltered in her womb or (if you belong to a different school) her penis; or being mother herself, either mother with a phallus, mother without, or both simultaneously; or the garments serving to protect mother from destruction; or being father's penis inside mother's vagina; or the need to protect father's introjected penis in mother's womb (of which there is inherited knowledge in the collective unconscious) from oral and anal attack.

To take on and separate out for clear viewing the fortune cookie metapsychology, speculations, fantasies, pomposities, humbug, absurdities, outrageous yet unchallenged pronouncements, marvelous suggestions, brilliant insights, and original and demonstrable findings would take a work of obsessive-compulsive scholarship I do not have the desire and patience to undertake. Few of the key words of our language are definable except by other key words which are themselves undefinable (for example, "narcissism is the cathexis of the self"); little is stated as a proposition that can be tested in the

The reader may ask if this is a study of pornography or of transvestism, for the matter herein shifts from the one perspective to the other. This in itself makes, then, an obvious point: that pornography, as the perverse subject's key daydream, is psychodynamically about the same as his perversion. It is the highly condensed story of his perversion: its historical origins in reality, its elaborations in fantasy, its manifest content that disguises and reveals the latent content. Without pornography, one can obviously still study the dynamics of perversions; but with pornography one has a special tool that at times will give clues one might otherwise miss. Especially helpful is the fact that since pornography, for its creator, is produced for money-making, he will be motivated in the highest to develop a daydream that is not idiosyncratic. If his pornography is to pay, he must intuitively extract out of what he knows about his audience those features all share in common. If he does not, he runs the risk of selling only one copy. He therefore has to create a work precise enough to excite and general enough to excite many. Thus, pornography is for the researcher a sort of statistical study of psychodynamics —a more colorful and more powerful method than the opinion poll that is sometimes foisted on us as rigorous research.

With the relaxation of laws that restricted the production of pornography, the market has increased; it has been financially possible for the producers to cater more precisely to the taste of selected readers. And so, where formerly all transvestites, regardless of multiple interests within the genre, had to settle for one story, each now can find varied forms designed more precisely to his

---

observable world but rather only by recourse to authority or manipulation of more theory. And even after taking these unnecessary risks, we are often left only with a dramatically complicated rendering of the obvious. The reader who wishes to will find the evidence in Leites' devastating, unread book (86).

specifics. Thus, not all men who intermittently cross-
dress and become sexually excited by women's clothing
will take the pornography quoted earlier as their first
choice. They say that in the past they settled for it, purchased every book that came out illustrating it, but did
not feel it quite fitted *their* case. So, for those transvestites who find the overt sadomasochism in that story too
intense, there are now available more charming stories
of the happy, shy man and the happy, competent woman
happily buying women's clothes and then the happy
woman putting the lovely clothes on the happy man.

The following is a story from a transvestite magazine.
A masculine man with no previous transvestic interests
has been told to dress up by a woman he knows.

> It was now time to get ready for the barbecue and Lynn
> [the man who is to become a transvestite] selected a
> flowery shift and a pair of minimal heels for the occasion.
> More time than usual was given to application of her
> makeup to her eyes and mouth. How she enjoyed shap-
> ing it into the delightful bow that nature had endowed
> her with. Unusual attention was given to her hairdo to
> make certain it was perfect and in selection of beads of
> just the right length for her colorful outfit. Millie [the
> woman who is encouraging him to cross-dress] dressed
> similarly, but added two artificial flowers just above her
> ears.
> "You look simply wonderful," complimented Millie,
> "and a more beautiful girl just does not exist. However,
> try not to talk too much this evening, but rather observe
> what the others do and say. O.K.?"
> Soon the two girls were mingling with the other ten-
> ants at poolside, and Lynn's first evening out was under-
> way. Millie noticed as she watched Lynn moving about,
> how graceful and feminine her friend appeared. . . .

Later:

> "What a wonderful evening," exclaimed the enthusias-
> tic Millie. "Bill is sure a charmer and knows his way with
> women! Did you enjoy yourself too?"

"Yes and no," replied Lynn. "To be honest, I felt left out of things and did not want to get myself too involved and possibly give myself away."

"Don't be silly, just be sure and be yourself the next time we are out. Still I can see why you might be uncomfortable," Millie replied, "though no one could possibly suspect that you are not what you appear to be."

"It's easy enough for you to tell me to be myself, but remember that the me that existed till two months ago was all man. Business and sports would not be the conversation expected of me with the men, would it?" retorted Lynn. "I can get along well enough with the women alone. God knows I've probably read as much feminine material these past months as they have in the past ten years . . . and the conversations that you and I have had give me confidence with them, but not with the men."

"Don't worry your pretty little head about it now," Millie said. "We will solve that problem also in time. Get some rest for we do have a busy schedule tomorrow." And planting a kiss on Lynn's forehead she left. . . .

Later:

Millie was fully dressed and soon they were chatting about the many small things that most women enjoy. When they were finished, Millie insisted on doing the dishes, so that Lynn could hurry and get dressed. "Wear the beige suit and that darling coral blouse you like so much," she commanded. "I don't want you to look too overbearing today since we will be out most of the day."

Later:

The ladies were soon seated and Lynn was delighted with the assistance of the waiter in seating them. During their light meal Millie told Lynn of her plans for them for the balance of the day.

"We are both going to enroll in the John Robert Powers Charm School where they will not only instruct you on makeup and clothes which you are coming along very well with now, but also in the art of conversation and development of your feminine personality. Most women

> who attend these courses are weak in this area also, and
> if we are to be in mixed groups again such as the barbe-
> cue, I want you to be at ease, and this should do it."

At the opposite end of the spectrum are the stories in which the sadomasochism is intense, placed even more in the foreground than is the cross-dressing. In this form, the story is so slam-bang instantaneous that it is often represented simply by photographs without text. These show a "woman" tied up in ropes and chains in uncomfortable positions, in fact a man in woman's clothes; but what excites in this pornography is not just the male in women's clothes but the fact that "she" is chained. With pornography becoming specific enough for each type of man, there is less need to buy the pornography of the past that was acceptable but not ideal.

I have the impression (there are too few cases for sureness) that those who, in their childhood, were treated less cruelly by a woman (or women) prefer a happier pornography in which frank humiliation or even open physical sadism is not a part of the overt story.

However, these varying pornographies have in common the evocation of danger (humiliation, anxiety, fear, frustration) surmounted. In this sense, all pornography probably contains the psychodynamics of perversions. There is, I allege, no nonperverse pornography, that is, sexually exciting matter in which hostility is not employed as a goal. Most pornography is aimed at heterosexual men, however, and since there are so many customers and since there is so much of this minorleague pornography, such literature is "normal" in the statistical sense of being congenial to many men. Thus, for most men in our society pornography consists of pictures of nude women and of heterosexual intercourse. That these forms are common does not mean that they do not arise as solutions to conflict, distress, frustration, and anger. If they were "normal" in the sense of being a universal, biological expression of un-conflicted pleasure-seeking, then nudity would be sexually fetishistic in all societies (which it is not), not just in those like ours where it is made tantalizing by frustration.

Pornography spares one the anxieties of having to make it with another person; the people on the printed page know their place and do as directed.

Although popular, pornography may nonetheless not be simply (though it may, especially in adolescence, be partly) a substitute because of lack of proper sexual objects. It exists because it fills voyeuristic, sadomasochistic needs that in some people cannot be satisfied no matter how many willing sexual partners are available. Although genital orgasm is the final common pathway for pleasure and for relief from the drivenness of perverse need, perversions often use acts performed on objects or parts of the body that simply cannot be fully relieved by orgasm (cf. 152, p. 316). Nongenital organs—for example, eyes, skin, anus—and affects other than love—for example, rage, anxiety, depression—can, we know, be erotized, but the tension cannot easily be released, as it can in the genitals. This gives, I think, an intensity, a compulsiveness—a hopelessness—to perversion. Analytic theory, which connects perversion to neurosis and psychosomatic disorders, has long since suggested that if erotic tension builds up in an organ that cannot adequately reach discharge, chronic cellular change occurs.

If in pornography sexual activities are somehow portrayed in which there is always a victim, who is the victim in pictures and descriptions of heterosexual intercourse? Who is the victim and what is the sexual activity in a photograph of a nude?

While much of the excitement in the pornography of heterosexuality may come simply from identification with the depicted participants who are displaying their agility (and who do not suffer anxiety or genital failure as might the viewer), it is also likely that piquancy is added by the primal-scene fantasy of a child getting away with something when he watches what he should not and perhaps a sense of superiority from being an audience and so not exposed to risk. The victims then are the "grownups," whose lack of omnipotence is proved since they do not know they are being observed.

Very popular are descriptions of a woman who starts out cool, superior, sophisticated, and uninterested but is swept by the precisely described activities of the man into a state of lust with monumental loss of control. One easily sees therein a power struggle disguised as sexuality: the dangerous woman who is reduced to a victim and the boy who, by means of the pornography, for a moment, in the illusion of power, becomes a man (106).

I have said that an essential dynamic in pornography is hostility. Perhaps the most important difference between more perverse and less perverse ("normal") pornography, as between perversion and "normality," is the degree of hostility (hatred and revenge fantasies) bound or released in the sexual activity. One can raise the possibly controversial question whether in humans (especially males) powerful sexual excitement can ever exist without brutality also being present (minimal, repressed, distorted by reaction formation, attenuated, or overt in the most pathological cases). This may be comparable to asking whether a piece of humor can exist without hostility (25). In humor the hostility is not simply tacked on but is a *sine qua non* (though not the only one). Is it possible that in nonperverse sexual excitement, unconscious hostility also is essential and not simply anaclitic?

Can anyone provide examples of behavior in sexual excitement in which, in human males at least, disguised hostility in fantasy is not a part of potency? We are already familiar with a similar situation in which hostility surmounted is essential for normal functions, for we know that normal development demands that infants be increasingly frustrated in order to permit the separation that will result in the ego functions and identity necessary for coping with the external world. This process, using frustration as an essential tool, creates a reservoir of unconscious hatred, coping with which helps determine successful or maladaptive personality development. Mastery, that most gratifying experience, often comes about through restitution for passively suffered frustration by creating fantasies, character structures, or modes of activity that in their most primitive form are brutal, but that, filtered through a process of sublimation, may end up far removed from the original hatred.

If hostility could be totally lifted out of sexual excitement there would be no perversions, but how much loving sexuality would be possible? The differences between each of the perversions, and between the different perversions and more common sexual behavior, may lie with the specific differences in frustrations and gratifications (often determined by society but applied by parents, especially mother) experienced in infancy and childhood.

A few words may be in order regarding the puzzling fact that attempting to sell pornography to women would lead one to starvation. Why? In the asking itself, not just in an answer, there is information. The question is like "the age-old mystery"—to put it in its ripest form— What Is Woman? Only men worry over the mystery of women; women do not, because they are not mystified. This does not necessarily mean that they comprehend the dynamics of their own sexuality but simply that because they experience it, it does not strike them as mysterious. If women wished, they could ask about the mystery of men's sexuality, which may not be so clear as some would have us think. We may take it for granted that we understand male sexuality because most of the work on it has been done by males who, experiencing it, need not be so curious and mystified.

In regard to the question why women do not respond
to pornography as intensely as men, perhaps the question is wrong. Men tend to equate pornography in general with what is pornography for them in particular, but,
for instance, precise depiction of sexual intercourse, although exciting, is less compelling for women. You can
sell a steady flow of pictures of nude men to very few
women for erotic purposes, but that does not mean
women do not have their own pornography—they do.
Because their childhood experiences in our society are
different, women need some aspects of their pornography to be different from men's. By now it is known that
women are full of their own private sexual fantasies and
are stirred by pornography (see, for example, 36, 69).*
Men, judging the pornography of women, make the
same mistake as when judging the pornography of anyone dynamically different; not stirred themselves, they
cannot sense that the material might arouse others.
Reading the romantic, masochistic stories that in recent
years have been the surface that excites women, men
might think it trash, since it seems so unsexual. It can
appear ad libitum, not recognized—much less legislated
—as obscene.

In addition, most of us believe (cf. 78) that, although
they can be stirred by pornography, women are less
voyeuristic, and voyeurism is an essential quality of pornography. Although some admit nowadays to staring at
men's pants, women are never Peeping Toms. This may
not reflect a biological difference in the sexes but our
society's inhibition of a little boy's right to sexual looking
and a little girl's training that she is not to permit that
looking, which implies to her that it makes no big differ-

*My impression at this point, before studying the question carefully,
is that fewer *types* of perversion are represented in women's pornography, which, besides the gentle masochism-sadism romances, seems
to consist most often of endless variations on the favorite-harem-girl-
of-the-Sultan oedipal-masochism tale or the supergirl-frustrating-
droves-of-roaring-studs reparative-sadism fantasy.

ence to anyone if she looks or not. It may also develop that, as routine heterosexual pornography becomes available to them in a more lenient society, more women will discover a taste for such products. To the extent that penises become a forbidden but prized vision for girls as breasts are for boys, women will be drawn to penis pornography.

I have stressed the obvious, that what is pornography for one person is not so for another with a different life history and psychodynamics. Looking at the repetitive, unvarying stories of transvestites, the nontransvestite finds his mind wandering and quickly becomes unable to read any more. One day I asked a transvestite to bring in pornography suited to his transvestism; he told me that stories he had already shown me that I had been too bored to read were in fact the pornography. Similarly, what women may find exciting in books and movies will make men in the audience restless as they wait for the story to pick up its interest again.

It is also obvious that politicians today, when legislating on pornography, will tend to define as pornographic only those things that excite themselves and as obscene only those productions that make their own gorges rise.

Societies fear pornography as they fear sexuality, but perhaps there is also a less sick reason: they respond intuitively to the hostile fantasies disguised but still active in pornography. And so, pornography will be loathsome to the person responding to it (who, in responding, makes it pornography rather than foolish prose); the word "loathsome," like "disgust," implies not only forbidden sensuality but also fear that the hostility may be released.

Chapter 6

Hostility and Mystery in Perversion

Other factors besides hostility, risk, and reversal of trauma to triumph—on which this study concentrates—are also necessary for perversion formation. A whole book on the role of unconscious and conscious guilt, for instance, would be invaluable. But there is no point in repeating what has already been established or in speculating on others' speculations; all those ideas will have to be background for this book's limited discussion. I wish only to underline that the study of perversion is the study of hostility more than of libido. This book does not—is not intended to—reveal a complete theory of perversion. My decision, for instance, not to paraphrase in depth the work of others on the importance of oedipal conflict in the creation of perversion is purposeful; it serves to save time and lets me concentrate on the more controversial issues of the preoedipal period.

Still, it will be useful to review briefly Freud's thesis about perversion and then continue our earlier discussion (chap. 2) of the arguments against it in this new day of advancing sexual research. Freud said that sexual aberration was the product of constitutional (biological) and accidental (interpersonal) factors. He felt that there

were rare cases in which the aberrant behavior was almost purely the product of biological factors and others
in which it was the product of nonbiological, psychic
influences, but that the greatest number were due to a
mixing of both these elements (24). Recognizing that
understanding of the innate factors lay outside psychoanalysis and was still beyond the reach of the laboratory,
his main interest—and his tremendous contribution—
was to discover how the "accidental" led to perversion.
It does so, he said, in the same manner that neurotic
symptoms are produced: an instinctual drive from the id
meets an imperative "no" in the superego or in reality;
this makes the ego create a compromise formation that
will (partially) gratify the instinctual wish while placating
the superego or reality demand that the wish be gone.
The "no" is backed with threat: Freud also postulated
that perversion was—to use my concept—a gender disorder; that is, perversion resulted from the attempt
either to prevent castration or, in females, to make reparation for the "fact" of castration. And so the oedipal
conflict and its resolution in males and females was part
of the explanation, and in time, some beginning elaboration of the importance of preoedipal wishes was also
introduced. Of the many additions and refinements that
filled out this explanation, perhaps the most important
historically is the concept of "splitting." Freud describes
how the child in a conflict between a "powerful instinctual demand" and "an almost intolerable real danger"

> replies to the conflict with two contrary reactions, both
> of which are valid and effective. On the one hand, with
> the help of certain mechanisms he rejects reality and
> refuses to accept any prohibition; on the other hand, in
> the same breath he recognizes the danger of reality, takes
> over the fear of that danger as a pathological symptom
> and tries subsequently to divest himself of the fear. It
> must be confessed that this is a very ingenious solution
> of the difficulty. Both of the parties to the dispute obtain

their share: the instinct is allowed to retain its satisfaction and proper respect is shown to reality. But everything has to be paid for in one way or another, and this success is achieved at the price of a rift in the ego which never heals but which increases as time goes on. The two contrary reactions to the conflict persist as the centre-point of a splitting of the ego. (35)

While Freud is speaking here only of fetishism, there is reason, both in what he says and in subsequent work of others, to extend the concept of splitting to all perversions.*

The Implication of Moral Responsibility

Before looking more at the role of hostility, I must take up a moral issue inherent in every aspect of psychoanalytic theory but especially visible in discussions of overtly sexual and overtly aggressive behavior: the problem of free will; it is at the root of the connotations of "perversion" and is also with us as we create theory. To explain pathological behavior as due to conflict and to say it employs such mechanisms as repression, denial, disavowal, or splitting is to say, via the concept of the superego, that willed decisions—informed decisions— are being made logically by "agencies" of the psyche performing the tasks for which these "agencies" were constructed. Much of this activity occurs unconsciously, which mitigates but does not end responsibility. That the conflicts arise at first from dangers in the outside world —the customs of a society passed through the neurotic idiosyncrasies of parents—again only mitigates the sense

*That is understood when, in talking of how the victim becomes victor, I touched on the multiple identifications—some of being the masochist and some of being the sadist—that simultaneously are present at differing levels of consciousness in the perverse fantasy. Another example is Williams' (154) demonstration of how splitting is used in what he calls sexual murders (by which he does not mean people who murder for genital lust but rather men who murder women, thus blurring for me the meaning of "sexual").

of responsibility. When, so our theory says, we are attacked by these external dangers in infancy, we *choose* to
protect our instinctual pleasures, disguise our real inten-
tions, fool the people on the outside who are the source
of the dangers, and distract ourselves so that we lose
(repress) our knowledge of what happened to us and why
we behave. Thus our theory of motivation mixes determinism and free will into a brew.

Complicating this objective (scientistic) view of the
sources of psychic motivation is our subjective, omnipo-
tent (narcissistic) belief that our behavior is not determined (our choices are not determined) but is almost
always of our choosing; that is the message of the strict
superego. In brief, then, whether consciously or unconsciously, the person believes he chooses his perversion;
so he feels. And thus, though the objective observer
might not agree, the perverse person is sure he himself
has created, connived, pandered, disguised, manipulated: he considers his perversion his own masterly production. Analytic practice is based on the thesis that such
insight can be reached—that the patient will come to
realize that he believes he has willed his own perversion
—if the analyst's technique is good enough.

In this regard, Winnicott's concepts of the "true self"
and the "false self" (155) are most helpful clinically and
a necessary advance over "ego," "id," and "superego"
in much of our discourse. But his concepts sink us
deeper into the issue of free will and determinism, for
the "true self" is seen as that dependable part of ourselves that does not falsify our fundamental knowledge
—it is our ultimate subjective conviction (omniscience)
—and the "false self" as an inner person opposed to
dealing with the truth. The "true self," then, is the conscience of the superego. As I have contrasted "perversion" and "variant," in the former one's true self knows
its own evil, which does not exist in the latter.

Opponents of the psychoanalytic theory of perversion

take an opposite, that is, amoral, position (the position is amoral, not the proponents). While they may disagree among themselves, they are bound in agreement, as we have seen, that aberrant sexual behavior is not the product of (moral, that is, superego) conflict.

Mystery and the Role of Hostility in Perversion

Let me add another factor that in our society is also a source of frustration, with potential for trauma in childhood: the mystification of the anatomy, functions, and pleasures of sexuality. With its punishments, its promise of adult marvels, its transmission of society's sexual myths and preoccupations (too often by parents' secretive, guilty excitements), this mystification may contribute to perversion, if too intense or bizarre. For it victimizes children, tantalizing them with hints of dangerous pleasures that, being mystery, forever demand but are beyond solution. For instance, the anatomical differences between the sexes may promote perversion —voyeurism—in societies that sexualize clothes and nudity. The pornography of nudes will be ubiquitous when a class—in our society, males—is unceasingly informed, openly and subliminally, from childhood on, that they may not look, but that if they could the vision would be astonishing.

Freud made it clear (24, 29, 30) that instinctual vicissitude is the result of hostility—of two sorts:* namely, that inflicted on us from the outside and that generated intrapsychically in reaction. Most analytic workers have looked more closely at intrapsychic dynamics of hostility when searching for the etiology of perversions, for that is the traditional analytic process of discovery. Hostility was found to be divided into that directed against oneself

---

*Of two sorts with which I agree; a third, which in its final form he called "death instinct," is too religious for my taste.

(guilt, punishment) and that directed outward (rage, revenge). Perversion was studied by analyzing the perverse.

Considering that the view only from inside the sexual neurotic, although of greatest importance, is not enough to tell the whole story of the origins of perversion, I have also been interested in the pressures, especially hostility, that were directed by parents onto their now perverse child. Understanding of etiology thus opens up; the perverse person cannot really see what his parents did to him, when they did it, or why. (Would not the study of etiology in all neuroses be improved in this way? Not a new suggestion, certainly, but one for which few theoreticians have shown much enthusiasm.)

From this perspective, which places hostility in the center, the perversion lies in the meaning of the act, wherein is hatred and a need to damage, not love, one's partner. Of course, we are now in difficulty, for we risk finding that there is very little, including much of heterosexual behavior, that might not have a touch of the perverse. Freud implies as much in his description of the oedipal conflict and the pitfalls of libidinal development.

These propositions are most vigorously tested in the least perverse circumstances; the major perversions do not give them much of a challenge, for there the dynamics are too visible.

In order to illustrate these dynamics and to test arguments that arise in retaining the term "perversion," we can return to and study more closely sexual looking,* one of the most normative sexual behaviors of our society. No analyst will disagree that frantic sexual looking, that is, voyeurism, is a perversion. But can one call the ubiquitous sexual looking of men in our society a perversion? Does that not ruin the meaning of the term?

An obvious fact starts us off. In societies where there

*I prefer to use that term rather than "voyeurism," which already clearly connotes perversion.

is unlimited nudity, no one is keenly interested in looking at the freely available anatomy. On the other hand,
in a society such as ours in which certain body parts are
proscribed, sexual curiosity is aroused about just those
parts. The subtleties and shifts in degree and parts proscribed create fashions in dress, carriage, fantasy, and
pornography. In our time and culture, looking is far
more intricate and stylized for males (sadism is the
mythic theme in masculinity) and being looked at is more
so for females (and masochism is the theme here).

Our subject, then, is mystery, a quality so important to
sexual excitement that the two are almost synonymous.
Such mystery derives from childhood and the con-
voluted way our society obscures the discovery of the
anatomical differences between the sexes. Our knowledge that anxiety is an essential element of mystery is
confirmed, as Freud showed long ago, in oedipal development and in those of its anxieties that derive from the
anatomical differences.

But children of each sex develop anxiety about the
genital differences; why the lessened sense of mystery—
and why less perversion—in females? To some extent
this can be accounted for by the restrictions against boys
freely investigating female bodies, these in turn based on
and magnifying the ancient fear of female genitals and
generativity. A phallus is dangerous but not mysterious;
the womb's danger comes from silence, secrecy, and
growth in darkness—which is mystery. But behind these
factors may be found issues which, arising in the first
months of life, are still active years later, buried in the
depths of one's identity.

Freud's version of the oedipal conflict is puzzling in
several regards (143), one of which comes up now. He
believed the natural line of development is that of the
boy, who, in the unconscious of mankind and in societies' hierarchies, allegedly starts from birth a heterosexual with superior genitals and status. If so, why are

perversions more frequent and often fiercely bizarre in males? We may find a clue in the mystery itself.

Let us look at identification. Perhaps no other mental mechanism results in the development of such egosyntonic, unalterable character structure. Also, identification is possession: another person, or at least an aspect of another, becomes oneself. That is the last state to provoke one's sense of mystery. (My body and those like mine are not mysterious; thus, for instance, is formed one of the bonds in some homosexuals for whom the mystery—that there is another sex—is too frightening to be borne.) The first object seized upon by the process of identification is one's mother, a person whose psyche and body are like the little girl's but so different from the boy's. He must learn of these differences and in time accept them. Then, to become masculine, he must separate himself in the outside world from his mother's female body and in his inside world from his own already formed primary identification with femaleness and femininity (61, 135). This great task is often not completed—and that, I most tentatively suggest, is the greatest promoter of perversion. (We shall look at this hypothesis at greater length in chapter 8.) In men, perversion may be at bottom a gender disorder (that is, a disorder in the development of masculinity and femininity) constructed out of a triad of hostility: *rage* at giving up one's earliest bliss and identification with mother, *fear* of not succeeding in escaping out of her orbit, and a need for *revenge* for her putting one in this predicament.

It is no news that mystery is exciting, and most analysts are probably aware that it is an element in all perversion. How does it work?

1. In the first year or so of life the child begins to believe he is a member of one sex or the other.

2. Then the anatomical differences between the sexes are discovered; attitudes expressed within the family and

in society inform the boy and girl differentially that this
is a subject of keenest importance (24).

3. The desire to satisfy oneself as to the nature, especially the appearance, of these differences is great because of the implications of danger to one's sense of
maleness or femaleness inherent in them. The genitals
are the only way anatomy communicates the crucial differences of childhood sex assignment. (Length of hair
may communicate these differences, and to the extent it
does, cutting it is seen as a castration threat. Breasts do
also, though for different beings: adults.) But the need to
explore so as to find out (that is, to end the fear that the
sex differences exist or are dangerous) is, in our society,
frustrated more in boys than in girls. To be more precise,
both boys and girls may be told it is naughty to look at the
genitals of the opposite sex or to show one's genitals thus.
The messages are subtly different, however. The boy
learns that no one is surprised that he does so; if he is to be
considered masculine in our culture, he is expected to be
a bad, cocky little sadist. The girl, on the other hand,
learns to anticipate the boys' trying and learns also that
she is expected to resist. These attitudes, inculcated in
each sex, are reflected in such automatisms as proper
leg-crossing or the skirt-pulling "habit" of cultured
women when men are around. So the desire to look and
the promise that it will be worthwhile are heightened by
the very behavior used to thwart it. The more hindrance,
the greater the overvaluation and distortion. One becomes very curious.

4. At this stage, phallic importance due both to a physiological increase in penile and clitoral erotic sensation
and to simultaneous oedipal desires and dangers makes
this curiosity even more exciting and frustrating. From
such fertile ground grows the fantasy of the female phallus, a child's attempt at explaining mystery that only
heightens it. ("In all perversions the dramatized or ritualized denial of castration is acted out through the
regressive revival of the fantasy of the maternal or female

phallus [1, p. 16]. . . . Castration anxiety and its phase
specificity to the phallic phase play the central role in
perversion" [1, p. 28].)

5. Chronic, intense frustration—an essence of mystery
—with the built-in threats if one tries to gratify oneself,
functions as a cumulative trauma. But to reduce the tension of the "instinctual" desire by sexual looking is risky.
So the mystery increases—yet, thus far, no perversion
because, thus far, no gratification. Perversion, as we have
noted, is made up of both danger and gratification. The
problem facing the child is how to avoid danger (punishment) and how to get pleasure (reward) which arises
from three activities: decreasing frustration, successfully
doing what is forbidden, and having one's body erotically stimulated.

6. An inadequate but at least partial solution can be
reached by the creation of a neurotic psychic structure
(unstable when expressed as neurotic symptoms, more
stable in character structure); "neuroses are, so to say,
the negative of perversion" (24). Sort of. More likely,
rather than being a different category of reaction from
neurosis, *perversion is an erotic neurosis.* With this aphorism,
Freud was noting that in neuroses sexually perverse fantasies are disguised, hidden in the neurotic symptoms,
while perversions express these desires openly. But others have since shown this is not accurate;* the dynamics

*A. Freud (22, p. 80) gives us "the well-known formula which covers
the formation of neurosis in general"—and it certainly also covers
most analytic theses about perversion, including mine: "conflict, followed by regression; regressive aims arousing anxiety; anxiety
warded off by means of defense; conflict solution via compromise;
symptom formation." Yet analysts keep saying that perversion is a
different category from neurosis; they do so apparently because of
the manifest pleasure in perversion and perhaps because of Freud's
early belief that perversion is simply the carrying into adult life of a
fixated piece of infantile sexuality. Gillespie (44; 45, pp. 129–131)
reviews this issue and shows how Freud, who first put neurosis and
perversion at opposite poles (24), in time (30) showed that "the two
extremes, in fact, meet in the Oedipus complex." Gillespie especially
emphasizes the contribution of H. Sachs (1923), who described perversion as a product of distortion by oedipal conflict, not just as an
unmodified component of infantile sexuality. Gillespie concludes that

of perversion and neurosis are really different only in
that the first leads to conscious pleasure and the second
to conscious distress.

Whether or not the solution goes in the direction of

---

the essential difference between neurosis and perversion is only "that
in neurosis the repressed fantasy breaks through to conscious expression only in the form of a symptom unwelcome to the ego typically
accompanied by neurotic suffering, whereas in perversion the fantasy
remains conscious, being welcome to the ego and pleasurable. The
difference seems to be one of ego attitude and position or negative
emotional sign, rather than a difference of content." If that is the only
difference and especially since most of the fantasy is as repressed in
perversion as in neurosis—only a fragment breaking through to form
the conscious scenario of the perversion—ought we not to drop the
artificial, theoretical dichotomy? All we would lose is Freud's clever
phrase about neurosis and perversion being negatives. Earlier (43),
Gillespie had distinguished neurosis from perversion because the
latter was due to splitting, considered a more primitive mechanism.
Since Kleinians emphasize that splitting is part of all people's development and since it is described as essential in all the patients on
whom they report, is it helpful to use splitting as a means of differen-
tiating neurosis and perversion?

We ought not to cling to a clinical belief easily refuted by observation: it just is not true that the adult perversion is the persistence,
unchanged, of a piece of infantile sexual behavior (24; 19 [for example, p. 358]; 46, p. 181), an idea Freud stated in 1905 but no
longer accepted by 1919. Glover takes a similar position: "I would
suggest that it puts the problem of the deviations in a more satisfying perspective if we regard them as equivalents of symptom formations which, like symptom formations, can be ordered in a
developmental series in accordance with the historical priority of
libidinal and sadistic stages and the amount of aggression loosened
by frustrations at each of these phases" (47, p. 156). Interestingly,
this contradicts his position that *"the sexual perversions of adolescence
and adult life* [his italics] . . . although more systematized than the
infantile components of sexuality, are of the same nature. Of the
[perversion exhibitionism] it need only be said that it does not
differ in any descriptive respect from the exhibitionism practised by
small children" (46, p. 181). A child's flaccid penis is the same as an
adult's erect penis? The child's fantasies are the same as the
adult's? Years ago, Straus felt (as described in 7, p. 21) that what
was added by the adult pervert to his infantile sexual activity was
"decay," a word rich in intimations of hostility. These last authors
also indicate that a child's hedonism cannot be equated with adult
lust. A baby enjoying playing with feces is just not having the same
experience as an adult coprophiliac over whose mouth squats a
defecating prostitute.

A last hopeless mutter: Of what practical importance is it whether
perversions are classified as neuroses or as something different?

neurotic symptomatology without accompanying clear-cut, subjective erotic pleasure depends, I think, on the *exact* nature of the subtle, complicated reward-punishment system each family, usually primarily mother, develops. In perversions—the erotic neuroses—the sense of mystery and danger is heightened because the child has been traumatized or overstimulated explicitly at the point of mystery: genitals or desires to investigate genitals. Fenichel suggests some of this when he says, "Individuals in whom castration anxiety is provoked very suddenly and intensely are candidates for later fetishism" (19, p. 342); he thus indicates, as had Freud, that perversion may result as a "cure" for anxiety provoked by the realization that one can lose one's sex. (See also 1, 53–55, 57, 58; 137, chap. 19.)

7. I have said that perversion is made up of danger, with its painful affects, plus pleasure, some components of which are relief and erotic sensation. A piece of explanation is still missing, however. When one is anxious about the mystery and frustrated and angry in attempts to fathom and end it, what converts these painful affects to pleasure?

Somehow the danger must be undone. Fear cannot in itself yield pleasure, nor can rage. Something new must be added to release one's body for erotic response. The psychophysiology of fear and rage must be shifted into new channels if excitement is to change its quality and its course from muscles and gut to genitals.

The end to the mystery (with its castration anxiety plus the more primitive fear of identity destruction) comes by the creation of the full-blown, conscious, perverse act (or fantasy of the act). In it the mystery is solved by such devices as the phallic woman, denial, splitting, avoidance, fetishization, idealization, sour grapes, phallic worship, theories of male superiority, and so forth—a wide selection of mental mechanisms and fantasies all of which serve to trumpet that there is

no mystery. They do so either by denying the difference between the sexes or, in stressing one's own superior equipment, by saying the difference is without
threat. (Greenacre, for instance, following Freud, says
the fetish "serves as a bridge which would both deny
and affirm the sexual differences" [59, p. 150].) Thus,
by believing in women with penises, one denies that
there is a whole class of humans who are castrated; or,
in turning one's fascination to a fetish like a woman's
garment, one maintains in the symbolizing equation
fetish = penis that the woman is not castrated; or in
finding males the better sex in all affairs that matter, a
man can say he does not care that women are penis-less
since he—fortunately—is not female. But of course the
mystery has not been solved; it still rests there, unconscious, ready. Each episode of sexual excitement en-
tices the return to the surface of the questions and
fantasies that are the mystery. The resultant anxiety can
now be reduced only by the perverse act, which, however, in its performance or in its fantasied state raises
again the questions in the mystery. And once again the
mystery must be solved. No wonder perverse people
can feel so hounded by their sexual needs.* The most
stable solution possible, in the face of the real threats
presented by parents and society and the new form that
these dangers take when incorporated into the superego, is the perversion. And, fixed indissolubly in
place by the experience of physical pleasure, it is all too
stable, so often unalterable by life experience or treatment.

As a first line of defense, children fantasy situations
that reverse trauma and frustration (thus fairy tales,

*Also at work, perhaps, is a reinforcing (conditioned) quality laid
down in contact with the CNS pleasure centers (113), adding to the
desperate, driven quality of the search for pleasure in the perversions and addictions. This does not contradict the analytic explanation, which emphasizes anxiety reduction. The two could potentiate
each other.

games with toys, movies, gratifying daydreams). In time, with modifications and disguises, they put into behavior, in real situations with people who do not consider themselves simply actors in their script, the action formerly only fantasied. Perverse people, however, deal with their partners as if the others were not real people but rather puppets to be manipulated on the stage where the perversion is played. In the perverse act, one endlessly relives the traumatic or frustrating situation that started the process, but now the outcome is marvelous, not awful, for not only does one escape the threat, but finally immense sensual gratification is attached to the consummation. The whole story, precisely constructed by each person to fit exactly his own painful experiences, lies hidden but available for study in the sexual fantasy of the perversion.

There are two hypotheses amenable to future testing, for which I do not yet have confirming data, that round out this part of the explanation. First, that the trauma or frustration of childhood was aimed precisely at the anatomical sexual apparatus and its functions or at one's masculinity and femininity. If the target was other, non-sexual parts or functions of the body or psyche, the result should be one of the nonerotic neuroses (for example, the compulsive personality when control, especially excretory, is forced on the child too early, too hard, or too long).

The second hypothesis is that sexual excitement is most likely to be set off at the moment when adult reality resembles the childhood trauma or frustration. This implies that more anxiety is felt during the perverse sexual act than is present in less perverse sexuality. This anxiety —anticipation of danger—I believe is experienced as excitement, a word used not to describe voluptuous sensations so much as a rapid vibration between fear of trauma and hope of triumph.

The perversion (that is, the newly created fantasy)

does more than solve the mystery, however. The central theme that permits this advance to pleasure is revenge.* It reverses the positions of the actors in the drama and so also reverses their affects. One moves from victim to victor, from passive object of others' hostility and power to the director, ruler; one's tormentors in turn will be one's victims. With this mechanism, the child imagines himself parent, the impotent potent. One no longer fears the mystery, or conscience, or the outside world. The perversion is one more masterpiece of the human intellect.† Life can go on, the child can continue his development, a sense of worth and the hope for gratification are preserved, and triumph is converted in time

*"The sexuality of most male human beings contains an element of *aggressiveness*—a desire to subjugate" (24, p. 157). "The fetish . . . contains congealed anger, born of castration panic" (59, p. 162). When writing of sadism, though not of perversion in general, Fenichel (19, p. 354) says: "Anything that tends to increase the subject's power or prestige can be used as a reassurance against anxieties. *What might happen to the subject passively is done actively by him, in anticipation of attack, to others.* . . . [Fenichel's italics] The idea 'Before I can enjoy sexuality, I must convince myself that I am powerful' is, to be sure, not yet identical with 'I get sexual pleasure through torturing other persons'; however, it is the starting point for a sadistic development. The 'threatening' type of exhibitionist, the braid cutter and the man who shows pornographic pictures to his 'innocent' partner, enjoys the powerlessness of the partner because it means 'I do not need to be afraid of him,' thereby making possible the pleasure that would otherwise have been blocked by fear. Sadists of this type, by threatening their objects, show that they are concerned with the idea that they themselves might be threatened."
   Boss (7, p. 21) quotes Kunz (H. Kunz, "Zur Theorie der Perversion," *Monatsschr. f. Psychiatre*, 105:24, 1942): "The inclusion of destructive impulses in sexual activities cannot be regarded as specific only for sadism, it must also be typical for all other forms of perversions"; but Boss also correctly complains (p. 22) that "no explanation is offered as to how 'destructive dismembering and deformation,' 'an action damaging to life' or 'the most evident destruction of the erotic meaning of love' (von Gebsattel) can be the sexually exciting content of the perverted action." That is what I am trying to answer: Where does the erotic pleasure come from?
†As with the other neuroses, it also serves evolutionary purposes in providing a mechanism whereby the species can survive and reproduce itself in the face of the trouble it (our cortical development) has gotten us into in granting us civilization (cf. 24, p. 156). See also chapter 12.

(when erections and orgasm are possible) out of disaster, so long as ritual (eternal vigilance) is maintained and autonomous.

In the sexual excitement now available is subliminal awareness of the reward and punishment consequent to sexual desire. And so, when excited, one moves between the sense of danger and the expectation of escape from danger into sexual gratification. Risk was taken and surmounted. Orgasm then is not merely discharge or even ejaculation but a joyous, megalomanic burst of freedom from anxiety (analogous to the release of great laughter following a beautifully executed joke, where the build-up of hostile intent is suddenly fractured, with laughter the outcome [25]). The line between explosive triumph and impotence is a fine one, however. The wrong kind of risk-taking (that which threatens to reveal its origins) withers excitement. No wonder change in the ceremony can reduce sexual excitement.

To remind us of the familiar, here is a prostitute talking about mystery and boredom after a year in the trade:

> The thing that bothers me about what I am doing is that seeing guys, seeing men's bodies, gets to be a bore. Part of the excitement was seeing a guy's genitals or feeling them. But I just don't get the same reaction now as I used to when it was more or less a mystery to me. I don't know if it is just because of the job—seeing nude guys all the time and participating sexually with them. Because sometimes I do get it off, even with my customers. Because a lot of them are really good looking, and a lot of them satisfy me. In a way, I almost use the working thing as an excuse for having sexual contact. The time when it is still good is when you become so totally absorbed in your self-satisfaction and you become so totally selfish.
>
> You have all these men and you see all these men; and at first you are really excited about them being men. That in itself turns you on and gives you orgasms, because of

just the sheer feeling of being with somebody. Then they
start to suffocate you. I have experienced every type of
sexual trip you want to experience, from masochist, sadist, everything; to women. That's not even men. But
now, to achieve an orgasm is like having to almost battle
for it; it no longer happens really easily just because of
the sheer excitement of it all. A lot of times, I get more
excited when I have my clothes on and he has his clothes
on and we are making out and playing around. I get really
excited then. Then he takes off his clothes and we get
into bed, and all of a sudden it becomes— Sometimes, it
is even funny. Sometimes I almost want to laugh, because
it is like a joke, like laying there and the guy is going
bang, bang—you know—bang, bang. A lot of guys I
might have been very unfair to: "Let's not make this an
athletic event."

I don't think it is my problem alone. I think that it is
men's too. Sex is so available to men now that they've
become disinterested in it. All it is to them is getting on
top of a woman and then getting it off.

The explanation for excitement in sexual looking
goes like this so far: When the inevitable curiosity
about the differences in the sexes arises in the small
child, the desire to look becomes intense, insatiable,
and permanent to the extent that the body parts to be
looked at are forbidden and at the same time considered desirable by the parents; in their forbidding, parents let their child know there is dangerous pleasure
possible. Therefore, in our society where the female
anatomy is the more forbidden, but enticingly so,
males will tend to overvalue and be excited by looking and females by being looked at.

Now one major way for the looking to be sexually
exciting—if the thesis is correct—is for a man to believe
he is acting forcefully, sadistically, upon an unwilling
woman: he is doing what, so goes his fantasy, she decidedly does not want. If he can do so, he defeats her; he
gets revenge for past frustration. Finally it is woman's

turn to suffer; the excitement in pornography requires a depicted victim, though the more normative the perversion, the less obvious the depiction (for example, a picture of a congenial nude female hides the dynamic more than a picture of a woman being tortured). Inherent in sexual looking is a desire to degrade females, to which women may respond with their own attack ("seductive" clothes, "provocative" posturing); the rules of the game at present in our society demand that this take the *form* (but not the substance) of passivity.* Socarides (132) has noted how "very often sadistic impulses are tied up with scopophilia. The individual wants to see in order to destroy by seeing; or to gain reassurance that the object is not yet destroyed; or else looking itself is unconsciously thought of as a substitute for destroying. 'I did not destroy it; I merely looked at it' (Fenichel, 1945)." (The envy of the opposite sex buried in this—in looker and lookee—will not be discussed here.)

We need not use such obvious perversions as rape, exhibitionism, sadism, or homosexuality for confirmation. We can turn again to the trivial. A woman in a drawing room treasures† the privacy of every inch of thigh‡ that might be displayed beyond her permissible level. But on the beach, the formerly contested vision is just skin, simply because the man knows she does not care there. Likewise, a strange woman is exciting, while for too many men the familiar is a bore. The sight he would sacrifice so much for early on quickly palls when

*Perhaps what we too often consider sex appeal in certain provocative women is no more than a compact packaging of the sadomasochism of exhibitionism, a guileful display of sexual vulnerability mixed with erotic attack via posturing, facial poses, and partial nudity. What are the girl's fantasies as she poses for nude magazine pictures? A fuller understanding of perversion may come from analyzing the perverse person's willing partners.

†Or acts to others and perhaps herself as if she treasures. Under certain circumstances, when she intuitively senses these dynamics of hostility in a man watching her, her own exhibition will excite her, for she too struggles toward revenge and triumph.

‡It used to be ankles; dynamics are more permanent than borders.

the man realizes the woman does not care that he looks. To repair this psychodynamically based flaw, women resort to fashion; design informs men there really still is a mystery, which can be penetrated only against resistance. Fashions cater to the man's fantasy that he might forcefully take what would not easily be given.

In the individual, this mechanism is perverse, that is, neurotic; in the society, normative, since the frustration is almost universally applied. (We shall touch on the problem of normative-normal in a moment.)

In this material, I want only to bring out this perspective of frustration by parents and its harvest of rage. What is oversexualized is determined precisely by parents; they do so in this process of frustrating (and in nervously underlining their own secret pleasure in) what would otherwise be, if they stayed out of it as is done in some societies, only a mildly erotic experience or attitude.

Perversion and Normality

The argument about whether to use the terms "perversion" or "variant" and "normal" or "normative" can be approached again here, I think, if we are careful. "Perversion" depends on a connotation of abnormality; yet I have described a perversion mechanism—or can we say "pervertic," a neologism reminiscent of "neurotic"? —perhaps used by all humans. So we are back with an issue that has been in psychoanalysis for decades: just as one asks is anyone not neurotic, some of us ask is anyone not perverse. Obviously, answers will depend on the matter of degree rather than being absolute Yes or No.

I should make manifest that "perversion" is used two different ways in this chapter. One way signifies a diagnosis, a personality state in which the sexual fantasy motivates the greater part of a person's behavior. The other labels a mechanism. Just as a neurosis is different from a neurotic mechanism, so a perversion is different from a perversion mechanism. While both of the latter serve to preserve sexual gratification against childhood trauma, in the first case (perversion) this trauma was an onslaught, in the second (the mechanism) a condition of a civilization. Either way, since the original sexual impulse must be thwarted, disguised, and reinvented and the whole process perpetuated, since anxiety and risk-taking, violence, and revenge are hidden in the symptomatology, one must use a word that connotes this intense dynamic tension. "Variance" simply won't do, especially because it is preferred by those who deny these dynamics. Still, for describing a ubiquitous mechanism, "perversion" is too strong; it cannot rid itself of moral taint. The very normativeness demands that one care about the meaning of words. To the point here is a remark of Freud's: "No healthy person, it appears, can fail to make some addition that might be called perverse to the normal sexual aim; and the universality of this finding is in itself enough to show how inappropriate it is to use the word perversion as a term of reproach" (24, p. 160).

Devereux gives us an important assist when he points out that foreplay (with its use of perversion mechanisms) serves to increase tension and to heighten one's involvement with a partner, while perversion proper aims to release tension and ignores one's partner's individuality. A review of Devereux's position says that "a sexual relationship in which the behavior is normal but the object relationship defective is essentially perverted. If this definition is taken to encompass the vast majority of human sexual relations and to place them in the category of perverted relations, Devereux maintained, then so be it. It may be regrettable, he insists, but 'only an infinitesimal fraction of mankind is capable of behaving and experiencing even occasionally in a mature manner befitting genital characters' " (14).

The term "perversion," I believe, is necessary—notwithstanding its traditional pejorative meaning and dictionary definition—for certain character disorders in which the dynamics of hostility force one to aberrant sexual acts. But it is logically flawed and clinically inept to say that, regardless of the degree to which a mechanism is used, the person using the mechanism suffers a character disorder or that those whose practices are decidedly not to our (the definers') taste are perverse, even without a shred of the mechanism. Perhaps we can think of the perversion mechanism (like all neurotic mechanisms) as analogous to physiological mechanisms such as fever. Degree is important; the quality and amount of other signs and symptoms accompanying the fever are important, as are duration, clinical course, variations in etiology, or success and failure of the mechanism in restoring homeostasis. *But the mechanism alone tells us very little about the total state of the organism.*

We cannot understand human sexuality (how tempting it is to say "normal human sexuality") if we do not understand the perversion mechanism. Perhaps what heat does for the body the perversion mechanism does for the psyche in human life.

The old nonquestion: Are repression, displacement, symbolization, inhibition, and so forth normal or abnormal? By now, we should know that they are mechanisms, not judgments. We probably do not need the word "normal" in scientific discourse; it serves only for judgmental communications.

Aggression

Grand discussions of aggression are in vogue, and great, tumid thinkers are surfacing to bring us illumination. Territoriality, Destrudo, original sin, animal inheritance, a midbrain not quite connected to the cortex, capitalism, class warfare, twisted molecules, male chauvinism: each supposedly explains man's viciousness. Yet we might do worse than return to the analytic study of individual cases for clues as to how aggression (activity) is converted into hostility (hatred and violence).

The study of the perversion mechanism and the perversions may help.

Chapter 7

Perversion: Risk versus Boredom

Now I wish to approach this issue of the essential relationship between hostility and perversion from a different perspective: to look at the function of conscious and —especially—unconscious risk-taking as a prime component of the sense of excitement and sexual pleasure in perversion, and to cross-check the thesis by looking at sexual boredom. As with hostility, risk is sometimes part of the manifest content of the perverse act—in the grossly sadistic or masochistic perversions—and sometimes only latent, as in the fetishisms. Risk is inherent in the dynamic of revenge. We have seen how one recapitulates in fantasy an original trauma or frustration, with a new outcome: triumph. Let us add now that this attempted reversal is hazardous; one might immerse oneself again in the trauma. For pleasure to be possible, this risk cannot be too great; the odds cannot be high that one will experience the same trauma again. Nonetheless, the perversion must simulate the original danger. That gives it excitement, and so long as one keeps control, which is easy if it is one's own fantasy, then it is a foregone conclusion (even if disguised in the story) that the risk will be surmounted.

Let us not be puzzled by those perversions in which,

in reality, great risks are run. We must be sure which risk it is that we are talking about. The risk that one will again fully experience the early childhood trauma is the primary one that energizes perversion formation, and for some people that is more awful than risking one's life or being arrested.

The Sexual Fantasy

Just as every human group has its myth, perhaps for every person there is *the* sexual fantasy (perversion?). In it is summarized one's sexual life history—the development of his or her erotism and of masculinity and femininity. In the manifest content of the fantasy are imbedded clues to the traumas and frustrations inflicted on sexual desires in childhood by the outside world, the mechanisms created to assuage the resultant tension, and the character structure used to get satisfaction from one's body and the outside world (one's objects).* The analyst has the opportunity to study this sexual fantasy and uncover these origins. And the findings of the single analysis, I have suggested, may be confirmed en masse: by pornography. Pornography is the communicated sexual fantasy of a dynamically related group of people. Rarely, the fantasy may not take a cognitive form at all but may be manifested consciously only in the ritual used for masturbation (105, p. 826).

In the opposite of sexual excitement—sexual boredom

---

*"It must be understood that each individual, through the combined operation of his innate disposition and the influences brought to bear on him during his early years, has acquired a specific method of his own in his conduct of his erotic life—that is, in the preconditions to falling in love which he lays down, in the instincts he satisfies and the aims he sets himself in the course of it" (28, p. 99). This compaction may occur in other states, when defense mechanisms are built into a complicated structure, such as the neuroses and character disorders. For instance, Khan says (74, p. 434) in talking of those with schizoid personality, "One could almost say that their defence mechanisms carry ossified within them memories of actual experiences and traumata which the infantile ego had no other means at the time of registering psychically."

—we can find clues about excitement. Aside from heightened excitement that is the result of changed physiology
(such as prolonged abstinence, puberty, or other causes
of shifts in hormone levels and CNS function), it may be
that heightened sexual excitement occurs whenever the
circumstances approximate *the* sexual fantasy. Is this
equation possible: increased excitement equals increased impact of (one's own) perverse elements—that
is, cruelty? Modest excitement (barring physiological
shifts) would mean, then, fewer perverse elements, and
minimal excitement or boredom would mean, then, few
or no perverse elements touching consciousness (they
being absent or inhibited). Yet, the key point is not
whether the fantasied or experienced sexual act has the
perverse elements present, but rather whether they are
really present, that is, able to act.

By "really" I mean something that requires a few
words. Take the use of pornography, with its inherent
perverse elements. The pornography industry is built
around the problem of protecting its consumers against
boredom. Pornographic material has a short half-life;*
exciting material quickly becomes boring (121, p. 28).
The pseudoexplanation is "familiarity," but that does
little more than give it a name. It does not explain why
familiarity, in most arenas of erotic behavior, reduces
excitement; without understanding the dynamics or
without having lived in the world, one might as well have
expected familiarity to produce greater pleasure; it
sometimes does with happy couples.

Sexual boredom is, I believe, especially the result of
the loss of sense of risk. So, even if the other proper
elements are present in the fantasy/pornography, it does
not work well unless one can still be just a bit fearful,

*This is also true for other sexual stimuli, as is known by many
married couples, rapists, habitual masturbators, shoe fetishists, and
most other humans capable of sexual excitement: variety of details
within constancy of theme keeps one potent while protecting one
from the rigors of intimacy.

uncertain of a successful outcome. (The same dynamic of risk applies elsewhere. I have mentioned jokes. And it is probably also at the bottom of art appreciation and the rapid dating of art styles; committed art critics, like connoisseurs of pornography, are honestly and deeply unable to respond to a different set of expressed dynamics. And within their preferred genre, they need a constant flow of works at the perimeter, where one can imagine himself at risk for experiencing something new. Their natural enemy, the artist, has, nonetheless, a similar dynamic, a need for mystery and simulated risk. At the moment, I would define art—like sexual excitement—as the search for [controlled, managed] ambiguity.)

I am referring here to two sorts of risk. The first, not usually central to perversion, is the heightened excitement some people get in performing a sexual act where they might be caught (breaking a custom, taboo, or statute); this is conscious risk-taking and is used to add sauce to a dish.* The other risk, more important to our discussion, is concerned with unconscious deposits of the oedipal situation, such as the mystery of the anatomical difference of the sexes. The unfinished oedipal conflict in the adult places the possibility of failure into the center of his sexual act. Sexual excitement (other than its purely physical sensations) is, then, the product of an oscillation between the possibility of failure (small) and the anticipation of triumph (larger). The perversion is the complicated path that threads its way through the dangers to triumphant sexual gratification.

McDougall (103, p. 378) has already noted some of this:

> In every instance the plot [of the perversion] is the same: castration does not hurt and in fact is the very condition of erotic arousal and pleasure. . . . There is always a

*Not always; sometimes it can be a major element in the sexual act, as in sadomasochistic sexual rituals or in those persons who hang or anesthetize themselves to produce orgasm.

spectator to this stage play—a role which the individual will frequently play himself as he watches in the mirror the production of his special sexual scene. [Think of the relationship of this to pornography, wherein the reader or watcher is the director, with the portrayed participants as the traumatized child and his traumatizing parents.— R.J.S.] There is an important reversal of roles here; the child, once victim of castration anxiety, is now the agent of it, the dealer in castration . . . ; the excited child, once the helpless spectator of the parents' relationship or victim of unusual stimulation which could not be dealt with, is now the controller and producer of excitement, whether his own or his partner's. In fact, many perverts are uniquely interested in manipulating the other person's sexual response [as the adults once did theirs; cf. chap. 5].

Since so much of development and especially of differentiation is risk, especially in infancy, I seem to have made my task too easy, on claiming that risk is at the core of perversion; it is at the core of so much of character structure and symptomatology—only we call it anxiety. But what I mean here is something more precise. First, we know that risk is not quite the same as anxiety. Risk implies that one has stepped beyond mere experience of fear or anticipation of danger and is computing the chances of success versus failure. And so a new and complicated effect—excitement—is stirred into the brew; excitement introduces the possibility of pleasure. Second, in perversion, we find that the anxiety is not some generalized state of oedipal alarm. Instead—I hypothesize—in childhood, one was truly threatened with a danger to one's sexuality: to parts of the body capable of erotic pleasure (not just sensual pleasure) or to one's masculinity or femininity. The dangerous person was aiming at—is felt as having wanted to aim at—one's sex or one's gender identity. The blow was struck at just those parts of body or identity that distinguish the sexes or at the freedom to use these parts in the search to distinguish the sexes clearly. This trauma was very severe, by which I mean (as with traumatic neurosis) that it was prolonged too far, or else hit too suddenly or when one was too young for adequate defense. Intensity, suddenness, and incomprehensibility of a danger that threatens one's psychic sexual apparatuses set one up for a perversion (1, 54). A perversion, I repeat, is a sexual—an erotized—neurosis. In the other neuroses—those whose primary symptoms are anxiety, depression, phobias, compulsions, and so forth—the attack is directed at other parts of the body or psyche, not those that distinguish the sexes. (Here, probably, we pay the price for Freud's insistence that sensuality and sexuality are the same in childhood—because they often converge. Had he not so insisted, the perversions might have long since been seen as just one category of the neuroses.) And in perversions, in contrast to the other neuroses, resolution is sensationally rewarded—by great erotic pleasure.

Perhaps when the trauma is complete (if that is possible), no perversion results; rather, a function is simply wiped out. (There are people, physically intact, who have never been sexually excited.) Perversion, one may expect, is the result of damage, not destruction; hope still remains. "Risk" implies that. Risk indicates odds for and against success; human ingenuity may find a detour or substitute or, on occasion, perform a truly creative act to lift perversion into art.

The original trauma and the struggle that went on, out of sight, for years of childhood till surfacing in the overt, genitally discharged perversion, are memorialized in the act's details (chap. 5). And so is the rage that trauma produced in the child and that had to be subdued if life was to go on. We can expect, therefore, to find fantasies of revenge against the traumatizer, primarily mother, sometimes father. (When perverse, we are less of a threat to others to the extent we differentiate the immediate object of today's desire from the original object, who frustrated the great impulses of infancy and childhood. Obviously, the more one equates one's immediate object with the object who originally forced one to create the perverse dynamics, the more dangerous the perversion. The man with a clothing fetish only soils his immediate object, a piece of apparel; a rapist or sex murderer has scarcely disguised—kept unconscious—the immensity of his hatred for his original object.) Therein lies another source of the sense of risk, for one cannot be sure that the subsequent representatives of the traumatizer, one's later sexual objects, will not, so one imagines, see one's motives (as do one's earlier objects, now residing in the superego) and inflict punishment for the sin of revenge. To spin out the sexual act and fantasy—to recapitulate the running of the risk—but this time without the old trauma being inflicted again, without the punishment for one's arrogance in attempting this audacious act (the perversion), or without the bound rage against the traumatizers bursting into consciousness, sweeps one to a burst of joy, the sign of which is the orgasm. (Freud [32, p. 154]: "The fetish . . . remains a token of triumph over the threat of castration and a protection against it.") Such patients typically describe their orgasms as being of the greatest pleasure; this could be an exaggeration to justify the perversion. It has been my impression, however, in listening to such descriptions, that the patients really were describing a most intense experience.

To summarize the risks pertinent to this discussion:*

First, conscious. What I am doing endangers me with society (outer reality and my inner estimate of that reality). If I am caught, there will be trouble.

*Other forms of risk, especially those with which we have long been familiar in our studies of the dangers inherent in the oedipal situation, shall be ignored now, lest this presentation become endless. To go over material with which many readers, especially analysts, are familiar would entangle the thread of the present argument.

Second, conscious. What I am doing goes against my standards (conscience). If I am caught, I shall hate myself.

Third, conscious or unconscious. What I am doing my parents told me was bad when I was little. Nice children don't do that with that.

So far, the risks are at or close to the surface, the ones people have always understood. They are not specific for perversion. The danger is perceived as stemming from being involved with forbidden anatomy: forbidden part or person of forbidden sex.

But then we get to the more primevally forbidden, and so we leave simpler erotism for hostility, rage, revenge, violence, destruction. The risks now are perceived as life-threatening to others and oneself (unconsciously in some perversions, consciously in the perversions we sense are bizarre; the sense of bizarreness is usually an intuition of intensity of hatred).

Fourth. I am filled with hatred and must not know it. Because they (the adults) so frustrated (mystified) me, my sexual freedom in childhood was taken from me. Not only were restrictions imposed on me, but—more tormenting—I was made responsible: I must sense the temptation and prevent my own actions. For all this, I am to love and respect them. Hate is wrong and shall be punished.

Fifth. My sexual desires are bad; my hatred is even worse.* If they knew its extent, they would have to de-

---

*Ultimately it is murderous. But when less than this, it is still awesome. To break free of that first object, mother, and establish oneself requires that a barrier be set up to help keep one from succumbing to the urge to merge with her. This piece of character structure may be sustained by fantasies of harming mother; again, a risky business. McDougall says:

> The fantasy which is directed to the phallic castration of the paternal image hides another which is the castration of the feeding mother. If the first wish may be said to threaten the individual himself with castration, the second produces anxiety linked to depression, to fear of psychic disintegration and to death.

stroy me. But this violence is mine, part of the essential me that is evil and yet must be protected, preserved. It is hidden in what I desire erotically.

Sixth. For all this that was done to me, I shall enjoy revenge, which too shall be in the sexual act. But if I aim to harm my object, it may sense that and do unto me at least as I would do unto it. And that is most risky, indeed.

Perversion is hatred, erotized hatred.

Safety Factors

Triumph requires overcoming odds, but if the danger in adult life were as severe as it had been in childhood, pleasure would be absent and thus there would be no perversion. So devices—safety factors—must be built into the fantasy to reduce anxiety and guarantee that the odds are decisively loaded in favor of triumph. Their traces are everywhere in the micro-elements that make up the perverse fantasy or behavior. Here are random samples. Take the fetish: it is absolutely passive and so cannot threaten, interfere, witness, or accuse; it can be attacked, dirtied, hated, destroyed, and yet it is infinitely renewable . . . The obscene telephone caller does not

---

These aggressive-castrative wishes with their accompanying anxieties are held in check through compulsive sexual behaviour which takes on the characteristics of a play or a game with rigid rules, and leads to a form of object relation dominated by the same defensive mechanisms: disavowal and negation, splitting and projection, instinctual regression, manic defence.

As in childhood the game functions in the service of mastering traumatic events and states, and permits the individual to play at things he may not carry into action (libidinal and aggressive wishes); it also permits of a reversal of roles which often takes the form of controlling the orgastic response of the partner, this "loss of control" being regarded as a castration of the partner, or a reduction of his status to that of a helpless child. He plays in fantasy at being the only one to enjoy the father's penis and the only one to enjoy the maternal breasts; in consequence he may possess and punish these objects. Thus the desperate sexual game allows the recovery in fantasy of lost objects as well as the erotization of the defences against the forbidden wishes. (103, pp. 373-374)

confront his victim and have to suffer the knowledge that she is only a human . . . The prostitute is paid to be agreeable and to indulge in acts she might otherwise spurn . . . The transvestite hopes to convert his wife to helping him cross-dress . . .

Clinical Material

The following case exemplifies how risk and revenge are formed into excitement in perversion. Even to this man, many of the dynamics of his hostility are obvious. (He is not a patient, and the origins of his behavior are unknown.)

He is a male hustler, that is, a homosexual male prostitute of avowedly masculine demeanor. He has an invariant method of operation in the street. Only when a potential customer signals interest from a car* will he make a move. Then he walks over to the car, but he does not touch it, not even to open the door. He simply stands and waits for his customer to make the next move; not until being invited into the car does he enter. He sits down, waits to be spoken to, and then, in apparent passivity, is taken wherever the customer wishes. He does not suggest the price, the length of time, the place, or the type of sexual acts but waits for the customer to request and then answers. Experienced and wise, he picks up, from questions or remarks, what fantasies will be enacted. When, for instance, he is to be an ignorant but strong, uneducated animal, the customer will indicate that by remarking on the hustler's physique, suggesting in a question that he works in a laboring trade; the hustler agrees and invents a few details to please his customer. In other words, he assists his partner in the

*In Los Angeles, because the automobile is a necessary part of life-style, in certain areas and at certain times of the day the standard operating procedure is for the customers to be cruising in cars rather than on foot.

latter's fantasy but establishes that he was hired and is therefore not the instigator. Rarely having orgasms while hustling and thus working many customers without sexual exhaustion, he can play at this activity indefinitely.

Yet to say he is perverse simply because homosexual is to miss essential details—and thus dynamics. It is important to note that *all* the foregoing is the perversion, not just the anatomical homosexual act. He reveals this when he remarks that whenever he is having trouble getting an erection—and it is important to do so or the customer feels cheated—he need only think of the foreplay to renew himself. The foreplay is the ritual whereby the customer shows a craving for him, the hustler, the labeled servant. (The victim, the inferior, thus becomes superior, the victor.) His greatest excitement, however, is when he recalls that money passed hands; sometimes, his sexual powers depleted, he will ask for payment in advance in order to have the vision of the money itself on reserve during the sexual act. He may even put the money out where he can watch it during intercourse, for actually seeing that money, which was given to him by the customer, is the greatest excitement. One would be slipshod to call the money a fetish, however; although it is inanimate and although seeing it causes him to feel excitement, it is not the money per se that provokes this. He does not get excited by money just any time, as would, for instance, a transvestite with women's clothes. Rather it is the *conscious* knowledge of what the money stands for that causes the excitement.

That excitement, stimulated by the sight of the money, comes from hostility. What the inaccurate observer would call passivity in this ritual is no such thing. When we track back and find what this man was thinking, we discover he is using the apparent passivity as an act of hostility, specifically of revenge. Every motion he makes, from the first moment of potential contact until the end of the sexual act, is a successful effort to force the other man to show need, excitement, weakness, and therefore dependence on the hustler. So the other has to ask; the hustler only complies or grants. The customer is sexually excited and in need; the hustler makes him a beggar. The ultimate sign of the customer's weakness, then, is the money that has changed hands.

The need for such revenge is so strong that the hustler must keep doing these acts; he no longer even rationalizes that hustling is only for money. He spends the greater part of his day repeating this behavior, and even that is not enough. He has episodes, lasting a few days, when he must collect as many men as possible; then he does not go through the added complication of the financial arrangement but simply quickly brings a man to orgasm in some alley or other hidden place and immediately goes to the next, doing this to fifteen, twenty, or more men in a few hours.

Even in the rare relationships he has in which he is seeking sexual gratification (in these first two styles described above, his own sexual gratification plays no part in his motivation), he has to perform each piece of sexual activity and express his excitement in such a way that he demonstrates he is less committed, less eager, less desperate, less involved than his partner.

He tells with chagrin of the very few failures that have occurred in the practice of his perversion. There are, for instance, the men who insisted on a refund, saying that he had not done a good job; or the man who challenged him that he could not get an erection, and so, knowing this man was stronger than he, he was unable to get an erection; or the man who, after going through an elaborate ritual to set up the sexual act, including bringing the hustler to a beautiful, expensive apartment (to demonstrate the customer's greater strength), said that he was not exciting but that the customer would be glad to hire him now for a reduced rate, $10, to clean house.

The hustler knows he is out for power; he recognizes

he has an advantage over most of his customers: he is not excited as are they. But he also knows this struggle for power is present on both sides; his customers are doing the same to him. He notes that hustlers are expected to be strong and dumb; customers need an inferior man for a sexual partner. (Once, in his days of innocence, not understanding the dynamics, he told a customer he was going to college, and the man immediately lost his erection and his interest.) He realizes, regretfully, that once in a very long while, he will meet someone who will outmaneuver him.

In other words, the power struggle in male prostitution is about the same as one hears from female prostitutes and strippers.

One sees here dynamics of hostility comparable to those found in nymphomania and satyriasis, wherein also (though in a heterosexual guise) innumerable partners are necessary for one to keep proving oneself superior. In all these situations—in all perversions—the sexual object is victimized, in that way aggrandizing the sexual neurotic. Since his infantile traumatic experiences live forever inside him, however, his triumphs last only a short while and must be endlessly repeated. Where the sense of despair and inferiority rides too close to the surface, one must repeat endlessly and rapidly, as in the man described above.

He says the relationship between customer and hustler ends instantly after the customer has been gratified, for whatever hostility was held in abeyance during the sexual act is loosed at its conclusion. The power equation has shifted; the customer no longer lets himself be humiliated. The rich man puts the hustler in a chauffeur-driven car—returning the sexual servant to the street—and lights up a cigar in his drawing room. Both end with remnants from the manic episode each has privately experienced; each is left pretending only the other was fooled and degraded. Each ran the risk of failure, and except in the sad cases of actual failure (such as those touched on above) each tells himself he has triumphed.

This man awaits suicide, he says, when his looks, forti-
tude, and sexual powers leave him, and when the attri-
tion from his frantic life finally grinds him down.

(Note: This man does not typify all hustlers; he is
struggling even more than do most to contain his rage;
his excitement from money and his frantic search for
partners exemplify this. His perversion, while sharing
features with others, is strictly his own—though that
could be said equally for the relation between every perverse person and the diagnostic category to which he can
be assigned.)

Some years ago, Khan pointed up these issues with
comparable clinical data that described a homosexual
man in whom risk and revenge played their essential
part.

> He scanned every nuance of feeling and tension in their
> [his partners'] face and posture until he had worked up
> a "colossal erection" in them. At this point his sense of
> achievement, triumph over, and mastery of the fetishistic
> object would be complete. He would now solicitously
> and compassionately offer to suck them and/or mastur-
> bate them. The excited helplessness of these uncouth,
> strong, aggressive youths had a specially pleasurable im-
> pact on the patient. Here a distinctly aggressive-sadistic
> element entered into his relation to them. He would
> secretly gloat over them: they were in his power. The
> more they got excited and frenzied with their sexual ten-
> sion the more imperturbably quiet and gentle he became
> in his manner. He would often compel them to watch and
> see him masturbate them and make them ejaculate.
> . . . He always had a guilty apprehension that this state
> of sexual excitement was not pleasurable for the youths.
> (75, p. 69)

Risk sets the stage for the enactment of triumph, although perverse people load the dice with each episode
heavily in favor of success; in the daydreams and their
extensions—pornography—risk is only simulated, and

so boredom quickly interferes. In the actual perverse act, however, risk is part of the reality, which, I believe, contributes to the greater excitement of such encounters.

Other childhood defeats and frustrations—nongender and nongenital—presumably feed into these dynamics of risk, revenge, and triumph. The tensions of each libidinal stage—oral, anal, and urinary, phallic, and finally the full-blown oedipal—with their biological demands controlled (sadistically, in the child's opinion) by parents, are struggles in which triumph for the child would consist of being in control while the other person loses control.* That, I believe, is the central issue in perversions. This struggle for control and its attendant risk may increase excitement, but it can be exhausting.

Again we can give hypotheses a harder test by looking at a condition, exhibitionism, in which this mechanism is less manifest; we shall find that it still takes little clinical skill—or theory-making—to see how the perverse act searches among the dangers for the right sort of risk to create excitement.

Why are exhibitionists caught so often? Of competent intelligence, not psychotic, aware of the possibility of arrest, and in many instances having already suffered severe social consequences, why do they persist in their dangerous behavior?† The explanations come

---

*I do not believe, however, that the libido theory of perversions as fixations, or regressions to points of fixation, at zonal stages of development—oral, anal, phallic—is of much help for our understanding. First, in perverse people there are fixations at all stages. Second, why perversion rather than another form of neurosis occurs is not explained, and the acknowledged failure to do so has thrown theoreticians back upon such speculations as organ vulnerability to account for the specificity of perverse acts, or nonmeaning, ponderous phrases like "hypercathexis of anal libido" as pseudoscientific explanations.

†The Kinsey group reports, regarding exhibitionists:

Of all the sex offenders, the largest proportion (72 per cent) of their convictions were for sex offenses, and conversely the smallest proportion (28 per cent) were for nonsex offenses. ... In terms of per capita convictions they are again outstanding ... and rank first in the number of misdemeanours resulting

when one looks at the structure of the perversion.

To do so, however, we must attend to part of our earlier definition that in sexual perversion one expresses preferred, habitual erotic techniques. Without this understood, the multiple uses of the term "exhibitionism" will confuse us, for it has other meanings: (1) the non-genital, nonsexually exciting desire to show off, in children or adults, male or female; (2) women's pleasure in showing parts of their bodies, including (less frequently than other parts) their genitals, in order to be sexually exciting to another, such exhibitionism not being an end in itself; (3) homosexual men's display of their penises for advertisement. Thus restricted by our definition, we find that exhibitionism as a perversion—the need to show one's genitals to another in order to get excited— exists only in males.

This man, married, overtly heterosexual throughout his life, unremarkably masculine in demeanor, with a masculine profession, has been thrice convicted for exhibitionism. Although he has been imprisoned before and is now on parole, he risks his marriage, profession, and reputation by still performing his perverse act once or twice a fortnight. This usually occurs following a humiliation, most often at work or from his wife. He is then driven into the street by a tension he does not sense

---

in imprisonment. . . . No other group approaches them in the per capita number of sex-offense convictions (3.12). With regard to what we term "specific" sex offenses—i.e., exhibition offenses for exhibitionists, rape of minors for aggressors vs. minors, etc.—the exhibitionists had by far the largest per capita number of specific sex offenses: 2.13. . . . In brief, the exhibitionists had committed more sex offenses (as measured by conviction) than any other group. . . . The exhibitionists are quite recidivistic. Relatively few (13 per cent) have only one conviction; about one third, the second largest proportion recorded, had four to six convictions; and they display the third largest percentage of those convicted seven or more times (16 per cent). A group that can boast more seven-time than one-time losers can be justly labeled recidivistic. (41, pp. 393–394)

as erotic, to search an unfamiliar neighborhood for a woman or girl to whom he displays his penis. He chooses strangers; he has never done this with a familiar woman. In fact, he is shy about being seen nude by his wife, who takes him and his penis for granted. (He says she does not respect him; she agrees.) He expects to shock the stranger and does not show his penis as a precursor to intercourse; he does not know why he does so, only that he is compelled to. On occasions when women are not upset but joke with him, pretending they are interested, he flees. But when the woman is angry and calls the police—when he seems to be running the great risk—he finds himself reluctant to get away fast. Although his fear mounts, it becomes mixed with a sense of confusion that slides into immobility. And when this excited lethargy persists too long, he is caught.

The nonexhibitionist, unable to comprehend, thinks this man is stupid. How much more odd then must seem the arrested man's mood while he is being booked: at the center of his feelings of disaster is a crazy, peaceful, pleasant quietness. I think we can understand this: risk has been run and surmounted; trauma has been converted to triumph. That he is being defeated by the police means less than that he has been victorious over the unknown woman.

Our mistake would be to think the police were the risk; they are not. They are, rather, agents of the triumph. The real risk, from the viewpoint of the perversion, arises from the humiliation earlier in the day, a repeat of childhood humiliation that has left in him a fracture line, a fear that he is not a free-standing, potent, formidable male.

And so the risk—the lifelong risk—is not that he will be arrested but rather that the humiliation will persist. Displaying his penis, he shows in the most concrete way that he has not been humiliated, that he is not castrated, that he has not been defeated by women; and it is his way of protesting—insisting—that he is still a man. We understand his behavior when we realize he is concerned with exhibiting his manliness (ideal self) rather than his maleness (anatomy). Therefore, the woman who is shocked, who becomes angry and, best of all, frightened, who creates a fuss, and who brings on the police proves that he has reversed the childhood situation. She is complying with a necessary part of his perversion; now she is the attacked one and he the attacker. Even if he is arrested, he is peculiarly tranquil because the arrest indicates—briefly—that in fact he does have a fine penis, powerful enough to create such a disturbance in society. We are not surprised to learn, then, that the rate of arrest in exhibitionism is higher than in any other perversion.

We should not be puzzled that the exhibitionist arranges the odds so that he is more likely to be caught than is any other perverse person. He aspires, not to safety from the police, but to safety from the inner dread of being an inadequate man. Arrest proves one is important; it is a victory over the fear of being insignificant just as is the hoped-for shocked reaction in the females to whom he exposes himself.

I repeat again: when we examine every last detail in the sexual fantasy, we will probably find that none is fortuitous. All have their place in reassuring the perverse person that now he is safe. This time, the attack on him, which is re-enacted in the fantasy, will turn into an offensive against his old vanquisher; this time, exact revenge will be meted out: the former assailant will have to suffer precisely those sensations that afflicted the child-victim. But the story must not go off the track, or, like a comedian whose hostility has escaped and is destroying his humor, the excitement of perversion turns into anxiety or anger with loss of pleasure and potency.

Splitting, Dehumanization, Fetishization, Idealization: Undoing

As Bak (1) has suggested, fetishism is the model for all perversions.* One who cannot bear another's totality will fragment—split (35) and dehumanize (67)—that object in keeping with past traumas and escapes; he may then isolate a neutral fragment—aspect—of that person and displace his potential sexual response from the whole person to the part that more safely represents that person (fetishization). When the process of fetishization is benign, as it is in foreplay or the variations of sexual fashions from place to place and time to time, the whole object is finally restored pretty much intact. This means minimal revenge and minimal risk-taking; unhappily, full sexual satisfaction without much recourse to mechanisms of perversion seems a difficult achievement for most.

Once the body part (or an inanimate, related object such as a garment) has been split off from the whole human object, one needs another process—idealization —for reinventing the new object.† The hostility (potential destruction of the object) floating around in the latent fantasies that energize the perversion must be neutralized and positively, pleasurably, erotically infused or there will be no perversion. At this point in the process, the destructive oral, anal, and phallic qualities so well known in the perversions must be kept within bounds. This is scarcely possible in states of dyscontrol such as borderline or overt psychoses, conditions noted for their primitive, grossly hostile (and therefore bizarre) sexual acts. Then we find that objects must be truly—not

*And long before that, Freud said, "No other variation of the sexual instinct that borders on the pathological can lay so much claim to our interest as this one [fetishism]" (24, p. 153). To what extent is sexual fetishization synonymous with perversion?
†Positive transference is another, obvious instance of this reinvention.

symbolically—harmed or even destroyed, soiled with ex-crement (or words), or slashed, wounded, and physically brutalized.

On examining pornography we found dehumaniza-tion, fetishization, and reinvention. Aspects of sexual-ity are chosen in which are focused the essentials of the perverse dynamics, for example, in the mildest of the heterosexual male pornographies, photographs of nudes. These reduce the actual woman to a two-dimensional, frozen creature helplessly impaled on the page, so that she cannot defend herself or strike back, as she might in the real world. Even if she has a dan-gerous look about her, that implied risk is negated by her imprisonment on the paper. She can be insulted, dirtied, forced to act according to the viewer's will, and remain uncomplaining, smiling, or even phallic—whatever is necessary—but immobile. And she is not only displayed, available for any fantasied sexual hos-tility, she is also idealized. She does no harm, she brings satisfaction, she is aesthetic perfection (if not, another picture is chosen), she is retouched, she infi-nitely repairs herself, she demands no revenge, she is absolutely co-operative, she keeps secrets, she costs nothing in money or time, she need not be under-stood, she has no needs of her own: ideal (cf. 42). No wonder she becomes a bore (121).

While it is more difficult to get the same compliance when actually performing a perversion than when ima-gining it in pornography or daydreams, the properly planned perversion still permits one to choose objects in the real world that can be dealt with in this way. Thus, for instance, fetishism (the use of inanimate objects), or the use of prostitutes (humans hired to act like puppets), or the choice of people, like the transvestite's compliant wife, whose own neuroses complement—that is, find use for—the perverse act.

Khan discusses how through the

technique of intimacy . . . the pervert induces and coerces
another person into becoming an accomplice [by estab-
lishing] a make-believe situation involving in most cases
the willing seduced cooperation of an external object.
. . . There is always, however, one proviso. The pervert
himself cannot surrender to the experience and retains
a split-off, dissociated, manipulative ego-control of the
situation. (76, pp. 399, 402)

(In fact, Khan's is an accurate description of all seduction, which is too often a hostile, power-seeking, fetishiz-
ing business.) One who turns his objects into fetishes
reduces his capacity for intimacy so that his own human
dimension comes to have no greater measure than that
of the fetish he creates (chooses).

Splitting, dehumanization, fetishization, and idealization result from failure of empathy and diminished or
inhibited capacity to identify with others. Or is this back-
wards? The natural state of humans may, rather, be no
more than a meager capacity for empathy, with analysts,
artists, saints, and psychotics having an aberrant hyper-
trophy of this masochistic mechanism.

Theorizing, quoting authorities, and a clinical vignette
hardly prove a thesis. Yet I believe if one applies these
suggestions about the essential role of self-preservation
plus hostility—risk, revenge, and triumph—to patients,
one's own or those published, the ideas will hold up.
This will be true in the behaviors in which risk is part of
the overt content, such as genital exhibitionism, physical
masochism, transvestism, compulsive promiscuity, or
voyeurism; in those in which revenge is overt, such as
rape, sadism, soiling one's objects with excrement or
words; or in those where both risk and revenge are hidden, as in that paradigm, fetishism.

Chapter 8

Symbiosis Anxiety and the Development of Masculinity

In the Introduction, I noted that my thinking about perversion grew from research on the development of masculinity and femininity. This present chapter shows in more detail how the two areas of study may be related in the earliest period of life and turns to the question why most of the perversions are practiced by men, not women. The development of women, from infancy on, is certainly full of trauma, frustration, anxiety, and conflict. The state of the art of psychoanalytic explanation these days is adequate to explain why women are as perverse as men, but it does not have available an argument why they are not.

One might reach for global biological answers—males *are* different from females. That can always serve as an argument in lieu of specifics. But I think fuller explanation can be found in the world of interpersonal relationships, in intrapsychic dynamics, and in the study of the forces of culture; only in defeat need we fall back on the untestable—biologizing.

Although the psychoanalyst rarely has the chance to observe it, there can be too much of a good thing. We spend most of the time of our practice and theory strug-

gling with the effects of trauma, frustration, and deprivation; we know that careless, inept, minimal, or hostile
mothering damages a child. But even the work of major
analytic theorists who have turned our attention to more
benign processes in personality development has not
fully warned us of the powerful effect too much gratification can have in certain aspects of development.

The primeval symbiotic goodness both mother and
infant experience may not only support but also threaten
psychic development: that symbiosis, if too intense or
too prolonged, can damage developing masculinity.
Even the most competent mothering throws a burden on
the infant male, and a mother who would try to spare her
son that burden can completely submerge his innate potentials for masculinity.

Two Theories of Masculine Development

Masculinity in males, according to Freud, comes from
three main sources: biological factors, primary heterosexuality (desire for mother) starting as soon after birth
as the process of comprehension begins, and identification with father's masculinity as the oedipal conflict is
resolved (24). A corollary of this theory is that maleness
is the superior state in the mind of mankind—the penis
the more respected sexual organ and masculine ambi-
tion and achievement the more desired activities for both
sexes. Another is that women are inferior, for they have
inferior genitals, and from the start they are homosexu-
ally oriented, their first love being of the same sex (33).

In chapter 2, I noted my belief that this theory is partly
wrong in that the second source noted above—males'
primary heterosexuality—needs correcting. More than
anything else, the mother-infant symbiosis measures the
mistake.

Let us run through the theory briefly once more, adding this factor of symbiosis. While it is true that the infant boy's first love object is his mother, there is an earlier phase in which he is merged with her before she exists as a separate object; that is, he has not yet distinguished his own body and psyche as different from hers—*and she is a female with a feminine gender identity.* It is possible, then, that the boy does not start heterosexual, as Freud presumed, but rather that he must separate himself from his mother's female body and femininity and experience a process of individuation into masculinity. Heterosexuality in males is an achievement, not also, as Freud said, a given; if this hypothesis can be confirmed, then masculinity is not the naturally occurring state Freud said it was. Some rudiment of femininity is. We must look to see if it is not so that the first, the primeval, phase in developing masculinity is a feminine one.

I do not believe that the sense of oneness with mother encourages even a primordial sense of maleness in the first months of life but rather that this oneness with a female mother must be counteracted. Only if a mother supports the development of masculinity will the oneness be pretty much overthrown as ego development proceeds. She will do this first because she wishes for and enjoys a masculine son; given that underlying motivation, she will encourage the development of behavior she considers masculine and discourage that she considers feminine, a process going on endlessly all the moments of the day and night. To the extent that she has less than warm feelings for her son's becoming masculine, she will communicate to him her disapproval of those of his behaviors she considers masculine. (We need not be concerned here with a definition of masculinity suitable to *us;* what counts is what *this* mother, as a result of her life history and present dynamics, responds to as masculine in her child.) The precise styles she uses to reward and punish his behavior will shape his disturbances in masculinity, in the same way as other mothering styles shape

qualities in infants that become character traits in children (for example, 17, 38, 39, 90–93, 95, 96).

If some masculinity develops—and it will begin to
show as early as a year of age—then the earlier hypothesized stage with its feminizing capacity will be covered
over; and, since the behavioral surface of the infant's felt
femininity does not show up before about a year of age
(that is, masculine or feminine behavior is not distin-
guishable much earlier), then that earlier phase will
never be manifested to an observer. To confirm the hypothesis that a protofeminine phase exists, we need an
experiment in which a feminine phase of earliest infancy
in the male is prolonged enough to be seen and measured. If we find such an experiment, we can look to see
what might have been done to create femininity that has
persisted long enough for us to observe it. There is one:
the transsexual male.

The Transsexual "Experiment"

I hesitate to report these findings one more time, having done so too often (for example, 112, 137, 138, 144,
148), but it will help the reader unfamiliar with the data
and hypothesis to review them again, for they are related
to factors useful in understanding masculinity and perversion. Condensing greatly, the following describes the
development of male transsexualism. (Female transsexualism has, I believe, a different etiology [141], not appli-
cable here.) The first factor in this construction is the
need to separate out from the many conditions in which
men put on women's clothes that one I would call transsexualism. Its essential feature is not, as others feel, that
the patient requests "sex transformation," for other
sorts of patients do that. It is, rather, that there has been
no significant phase in life that either this anatomically
normal male or an observer could recognize as masculine. (There are rudiments, built on the transsexual's

knowledge that he was and always shall be anatomically male and that his mother, who gave him a masculine name, never denies his maleness [148]). Thus, from those days of childhood when any sort of gender behavior makes its first appearance, this boy has appeared as if he believed himself a girl (not a *female* but a *girl*). His behavior has always been feminine; and in it there has been no more quality of imitating or acting than in undeniably feminine girls. The behavior in the boys treated, from age four or five* into adulthood, springs from a feeling of femininity expressed as the conviction that one ought to be a female (although transsexuals do not actually claim they are females; they recognize their anatomy as male). There is no effeminacy in their behavior, from earliest childhood on (effeminacy here implies mimicry or caricature, in other words a hostility and envy toward women that has to be minimized or denied; femininity here implies naturalness and no caricature). Rather, transsexuals have a conscious, open, undefended envy, comparable to that of a person born without limbs toward those more fortunate. The naturalness of this femininity is noted by all observers: family, relatives, peers, neighbors, teachers, strangers, and us who observe the transsexual child and adult in our research. By the time these boys are three or four, strangers are already confusing them with girls, regardless of the clothes worn. When playing, these boys wish to do as if they were girls; they take only girls' roles and are accepted almost immediately by girls when playing girls' games from which other boys are excluded. As childhood progresses and passes into adolescence and adulthood, the femininity does not diminish, the desire to have a female body persists, and no amount of threat can

---

*I have seen none younger, but my colleague, Green, has recently been studying larger numbers of feminine boys, not necessarily transsexuals, for his research (52); four out of forty-five have been ages three to four.

make the transsexual able even to imitate a masculine person for a few moments (137).

The condition is rare, far rarer than the number of patients requesting "sex change." Perhaps for this reason, theoreticians state that transsexuals are not as those described above. Except for mine, in almost all papers written on male transsexualism, clinical data are reported revealing episodes or long stretches of time in which the patient looked masculine, behaved in a masculine manner, and had heterosexual experiences or overt sexual perversions, and other signs that the femininity was not of the same sort as that reported above. This should be emphasized: almost all men have profound feelings for, concern about, and pleasure from their genitals. These organs are both a direct source of sensations and a confirmation that one's sex assignment is correct, his gender identity inevitable, and his masculinity valuable. If these positions are threatened, almost all males will set up defenses—but not true transsexuals. They simply do not want, need, or cherish their male genitals, and they make no effort to preserve these organs in reality or symbolically. Perversion, on the other hand, is intensely sought-for, a preferred gratification of those very genitals, not a rejection of them.

Only with the foregoing picture are the following etiological factors present, and, conversely, only with the following etiological factors will one also see this sort of femininity.* I have found the following in all cases that fulfill the clinical criteria given above for male transsexualism; whenever these factors show up in weaker form or when some are missing, the degree of femininity is less, and the patient no longer has the appearance of the classic transsexual.

*There is, however, another type of marked femininity in boys, even rarer, I believe, than that described above, in which the mother consciously sets out to feminize her son, having wished for a girl throughout the pregnancy and having given the boy a bisexual name to mark her wish that he had been a girl (147).

First the mother. In her own childhood, she had little sense of worth for her femaleness and femininity. Her own mother treated this girl as if she were a neuter; her father, more admiring, encouraged her to identify with his masculine interests. Between early childhood and puberty, the girl so accentuated the masculine qualities that she wished to be a male and for several years dressed only in boys' clothes, had her hair cut like a boy, and played games only with boys, competing with them successfully and as an equal, especially in athletics.

With the onset of the physical changes of adolescence, the girl—unlike female transsexuals, whom she had resembled to this point—gave up all hopes that she would ever become a male. Instead, she put on a feminine façade and in time married. The man she married —the transsexual's father—is a passive, distant, though usually not effeminate man, who is not to be a forceful or significant figure in the marriage. He is expected to support his family and then simply offer himself up to his wife as an object for derision.

Into this miserable marriage, the transsexual-to-be is born. Yet, although the dynamics of the family are as sketched above, transsexualism does not occur in any of the children unless a male is born who is perceived by his mother as beautiful and graceful. This infant is the best thing that has ever happened to his mother. Finally, after years of quiet hopelessness, without a sense of worth about her sex or gender identity, filled with hatred and envy for males, who have what she wanted and was forced to give up hope for, she has created a piece of herself, from out of her own body and as if parthenogetically without the need of a husband, the best of herself, her own ideal—the perfect phallus. This boy will not have the envied and hated rub of masculinity; that, she feels, is guaranteed from birth on by his physical beauty, augmented by a lush nursing experience in which he is a fine feeder who enjoys his mother's body. The blissful

symbiosis is established from birth, and it is maintained
fiercely by this mother, for she has enfolded within her
now the cure for her lifelong hopeless sadness. Joy is the
energy that permits her—forces her—to maintain excessively close body and psychic contact with this infant for
too many hours a day and for years. By creating this
symbiosis, she binds—incorporates—her son into herself as much as one physically can. By identifying with
him, she tries to undo her own traumatic infancy, to
replace her evil mother; the present mother and infant
are to be all good. The bliss created in the symbiosis thus
becomes the aura of a new, idealized, perfect mother for
her.

When these families are first seen, with the boys four
or older, mother and son are still too intimate, touch
each other too much, and enjoy each other's company
too much, understand each other without talking. (This
has no erotic quality for either mother or son [60, 61]).
It is not as absolute as in infancy, for, while these mothers wish to be too close to their child, they *do* allow other
ego functions to develop, such as mobility, talking, reading, and the like. The closeness seems to be maintained
in a precise sector, that concerned with the passage of
femininity.* We also note the power of the symbiosis
when we try to treat mother and son, with treatment's
implication that the symbiosis should end and masculinity supervene. Both resist fiercely (112, 148). Father, as one would anticipate, does not take part but
remains dimly in the background.

*In other words, a focal symbiosis. "By *focal symbiosis* I mean a
condition in which a symbiotic relationship exists in respect to the
functioning of a special organ or body area. [To this I would add: or
psychic function or identity theme.] Usually the individuals par-
ticipating in this symbiotic relationship are of uneven development:
parent and child, older and younger siblings, or even stronger and
weaker twins. The focal symbiosis represents the special site of emotional disturbance in both members of the symbiotic pair. But it is
ordinarily manifest in the weaker or smaller partner, who remains
functionally dependent in this specific area on the active response of
the other partner, far beyond the maturational period at which the
special function would ordinarily become autonomous" (56).

What is father's role as merging of mother and son persists and as the feminine behavior surfaces? He is to be absent and therefore to be scorned. He is scarcely seen—literally—by his son during the first few years of life. Father leaves home for work before the boy awakes and returns after his son is in bed. On the weekends, he is not with the family because, encouraged by his wife, he is allowed to spend the weekend solitarily, at hobbies or watching television.

The oedipal situation that develops further confirms the oddity of this symbiosis. Its outstanding feature is lack of conflict. The boy never develops a heterosexual relationship with his mother (without treatment) and as a result never develops an oedipal conflict. The two of them are so much one, are so free upon each other's bodies, that no sexual tension develops. The boy does not desire his mother as a separate, opposite-sex object, and she has no sexual desire for him. (Her lack of interest in his becoming masculine exemplifies this.) Only with treatment and the beginning of masculinity does one see oedipal conflict and the neurotic symptomatology of childhood with which we are familiar when we think of oedipal conflict (60, 61, 112).

The Pathogenecity of "Latent Homosexuality"

This review of the transsexual situation serves to demonstrate forces that produce femininity in a male. It is, I believe, correct (though one must be cautious, for not enough families have been studied to test it) that when all these factors are present and strong, the femininity will be greatest. As one reduces the intensity of the factors or as factors drop out, the femininity is less pure. I therefore extrapolate to a belief that at least a minimum tendency toward transsexualism occurs in the usual masculine state. And that brings us home to principles enunciated by Freud as early as 1905, never repudiated in his theory or in his clinical observations, that bisexuality (homosexuality, masculine protest, fear of females) is part of the make-up of men. The only difference is that what we call at present "transsexual" he labeled "homo-. sexual." (By no means is this the only meaning he gave to "homosexual.") Let us carry these ideas further.

In his last statement regarding the sexuality of men and women, Freud said he could never resolve in either sex their "masculine protest," that is, men's need to insist on their masculinity and to fear attack upon it and women's need to react with penis envy and its permutations to the effects of imagined castration (34). These ideas he attributed to "latent homosexuality," another manifestation of which was the forbidden—unconscious or conscious—wish for sexual pleasure with a person of the same sex. He found dread of homosexuality to be pathogenic in many major diagnostic conditions, and his closest followers extended the list until that factor was raised to being a cause in all psychic disorder. In time, it was carefully scrutinized, clinicians and theoreticians finding it too grand an explanation. Some suggested homosexuality was in itself a defense rather than an underlying cause (82, 123); others emphasized that male homosexuality, which seemed to Freud to spring primarily from a son's disturbed relationship with his father, could be traced back to preoedipal disturbances in mother-son relationships (153, 3, 130).

In perhaps his greatest exposition of the role of latent homosexuality in causing illness, the Schreber case, Freud felt he demonstrated the etiology of paranoid states, including psychosis, to be dread of homosexuality; he saw homosexuality in males especially as a pathology of the resolution of a boy's oedipal conflict with his father (27). This idea has subsequently been well criticized by those emphasizing the role of frustration, trauma, and conflict in the earliest stages of life. With these later workers the mother-infant relationship moves to the fore of the explanation. Some (125, 153) suggest that within the violent, hostile potentials of the oral stage there is also embedded in Schreber and by extension in other psychotics, as well as in those overtly homosexual, a desire to merge again with mother. For our present purpose, we can note, as did MacAlpine and Hunter years ago (88), that what Freud called Schreber's homosexuality is in fact a surge of transsexual impulses: Schreber's body is changing to female. And that impulse is one of the sources of the dread of homosexuality, which might better be called "dread of transsexualism."

These latter modifications, with which I agree, push the pathogenic conflicts back toward earliest infancy. They all emphasize that bad mothering, innate defects in the infant, or both traumatically disrupt what should be a happy symbiosis. Still, it is well to recall also that, for many infants, there are nonconflictual, nondefensive aspects of this merging: for some, the experience was often simply marvelous. Not all infants have the same symbiotic experience with their mothers. For some it is bitter —and they are thus in danger. But for some it is joyous. Yet to the extent it is the latter, even these fortunate infants may be at risk, for a dangerous remnant is left behind as the boy works his way out of the symbiosis toward masculinity. In other words, for males, not only is a deprived symbiosis a threat to development but so, in a different way, is good-enough mothering, and more so, too-gratifying mothering. By pointing up this nonconflictual aspect, perhaps I can draw the concept of merging from the special case of psychopathology to the general one of normative psychology. The transsexual is our bridge.

We have seen how a disturbed, unhappy mother, with a need to preserve the one experience of goodness she has ever had, will make superhuman efforts to prevent pain, frustration, trauma, and conflict from developing in her infant. She surrounds him with the pleasures of

her all-giving body, never letting go of him because of
the good feelings his presence produces in her and her
wish to protect him from experiencing the bad infancy
and childhood to which she was exposed. We have followed the argument that normal mothering in the best
circumstances follows a similar pattern, though of less
intensity and duration (cf. 155). We know that in good-
enough mothering, episodes of blissful merging occur.
Therefore, it may be that imbedded in every male there
remains, even as the years pass, at least a trace of that
earliest merging, a "primary identification" with his
female mother and therefore with her femaleness and
femininity. (The quotes indicate my belief that there is
more to this process, especially in its earliest stages, than
what is usually called identification; see below: the "biopsychic." "The infant's dependence on the mother . . .
does not involve identification; identification being a
complex state of affairs inapplicable to the early stages
of infancy" [155, p. 301].) The same tendency for merging in a female need not be a threat to gender identity;
it only augments or at least helps sustain femininity in
her.

Gender Symbiosis

Gender symbiosis is the aspect of the symbiosis that
transmits to and from infant and mother attitudes and
information about both partners' masculinity and
femininity. Unfortunately, the mechanisms that keep an
infant thus attached are not yet understood. Psychoanalytic theories need, I think, some of the findings and
concepts of learning theorists; these, although as yet
rudimentary in research on humans, can at least help us
speculate—as follows.

These mechanisms, in the first months of life, are "biopsychic," by which I mean that stimuli from the environment (and probably less sharply sensed stimuli from the

inner environment, such as pain or proprioception) set up changes in the nervous system that function (more or less) permanently as neurophysiological sources of motivation, the change now serving as a nonmental "memory." (The quotation marks indicate that this is psychologically a different experience from what is commonly called memory; how it might be related physiologically to psychic memory has not yet been worked out.) Examples are imprinting, classical conditioning, visceral conditioning, and perhaps certain forms of operant conditioning.

By nonmental I mean that the stimuli and the changes they bring have no psychic representation and never did. These new foci for behavior therefore are not remembered, in the ordinary sense of the word, nor are they felt by any of the senses. They cannot be recalled, for they never existed as part of mental life. They are more silent than what is commonly meant by "unconscious" and are a different category to be added to what Freud referred to as the sources of "drives" ("instincts") (29). They are as silent, as, say, the effects of hormones.* (See the discussion in chapter 6 on free will and determinism.)

If these notions apply to research on infantile development, then personality development cannot be fully understood by means of the technique used in a psychoanalysis. As Racker says (119, p. 79), "The study of transference has been one of the most important sources of knowledge regarding the child's psychological processes." Exactly: processes, but not actual experiences. Freud hints of this in his warning that often egosyntonic character structure is beyond modification by psychoanalysis (34). We need minute, systematized observation

---

*I am in no way suggesting that these nonmental forces, the province especially of learning theorists, are all there is to early psychic development. As time passes and object representations, under the influence of drives, gather into memories and fantasies, mother's influence helps cause her infant's learning to become enriched, cognitive, mental.

of infantile behavior in its natural state, which especially includes mother, the ambiance she creates, and those of her attitudes and behavior that touch her infant, to provide us with more information about personality development.

With this detour, I am suggesting a flimsy but perhaps someday usable framework on which to hang experimental data, observations, and theory about earliest stages of psychic development. At present, the framework serves me as a rationalization, a comfort in this period of little data, to "explain," in the transsexual, the transmission of mother's femininity into her infant son so that by around a year (more or less) he openly behaves in a feminine manner. In fact, of course, the only data we have now are that a mother with a particular form of bisexuality and a father with an intense passivity and inability to be close to his son have a beautiful and graceful infant who stimulates this mother to set up an excessively close and blissful symbiosis from which the rest of the world is excluded for too long. Then, at the time when first gender behavior can be measured, it is feminine. There are no other data yet. What happens inside that symbiosis has not yet been seen grossly or microscopically, and so I have shoved into that vacuum this theoretical framework.

But this theory is not crucial for our main argument regarding the role of symbiosis anxiety in creating masculinity. For that, it is sufficient to say that the urge to return to a state of oneness with mother, long known to analysts, remains as a permanent fundament of character structure and, depending on one's life experience after infancy, may serve as a stronger or weaker locus of fixation for regression. (It is probably latent in every "act" of regression.) I am only emphasizing now—again, what is well known from Freud's early works on—that such regression is often accompanied by what he called "homosexuality" and what I think of as "a transsexual tendency." We recall the finding that fear of changing sex is ubiquitous (some say universal) in male psychotics but infrequent in females (whose delusional-hallucinatory systems, when sexual, are most often heterosexual [62, 79, 81, 107]). We also observe that in the general population—in most cultures and most eras about which we have information—men seem more concerned to preserve their masculinity against real or imagined insult than women their femininity.

Symbiosis Anxiety

Symbiosis anxiety, then, is the fear that one will not be able to remain separate from mother. Let us now look more closely at that fear and see how it contributes to the development of masculinity. The argument begins with the observation that the ever-present memory of oneness with mother acts like a magnet, drawing one back toward repeating the blissful experience against mother's body. This, however, is a risky business for one who has struggled and attained independence from her. It is especially risky if one aspect of that independence is those behaviors called masculinity. A vital part of the process of separating from mother, then, is release from her female body and feminine psyche.

The ubiquitous fear that one's sense of maleness and masculinity are in danger and that one must build into character structure ever-vigilant defenses against succumbing to the pull of merging again with mother, I shall call symbiosis anxiety. While ostensibly set up to protect us from outer threats and insults, it must ultimately be established against our own inner, primitive yearning for oneness with mother.* If this is so, then the dim outlines appear of a major factor in creating masculinity, so intertwined with other contributing factors that by the time

---

*In women as well as men, though in women fear of being like mother in body and gender identity is usually not a danger.

behavior called masculine begins to be manifest (at a year or so of age), the masculinity is already inextricably tangled with the effects of symbiosis anxiety. The latter, potentiated by the biological forcefulness of maleness (in fish, lizards, rats, monkeys, and man), produces the greater aggressiveness and competitiveness seen in males as compared with females. This is to suggest that masculinity as we observe it in boys and men does not exist without the component of continuous pushing away from mother, both literally in the first years of life and psychologically in the development of character structure that forces the inner mother down and out of awareness. I shall no more than mention the idea that mother, in her representation as an evil, hated creature, may also lend herself to the task of permitting the symbiosis-mother to be repressed; one would hardly wish to merge with a witch. One can wonder if at its most primitive level, perversion is that ultimate in separations, mother murder (more than, as Freud may have felt, father murder). It would be ironic if some of the forms that masculinity takes, some of its strength, insistence, fierceness—machismo—*require* anlagen of femininity; the potential to be feminine is an unacceptable temptation that must be resisted by behavior and attitudes that society labels "masculine." Perhaps it is clearer, then, why most men seem so sensitive about their masculinity.

Greenson, in treating a transsexual boy whose mother I analyzed, came to similar conclusions. He talks of "disidentifying" from mother. It is not proper to cite Greenson's work as objective confirmation, since we have worked together for years, but his clear exposition, already published some years ago, is worth our attention. (I retain his bibliographic citations for their use to the present reader.)

> It is my clinical impression that the dread of homosexuality in the neurotic, which is at bottom the fear of losing

one's gender identity, is stronger and more persistent in men than women (Greenson, 1964). . . . I believe that we would all agree that in early infancy both girls and boys form a primitive symbiotic-identification with the mothering person on the basis of the fusion of early visual and tactile perception, motor activity, introjection and imitation (Freud, 1914, 1921, 1923, 1925; Fenichel, 1945; Jacobson, 1964). This results in the formation of a symbiotic relationship to the mother (Mahler, 1963). The next step in the development of ego functions and object relations is the differentiation of self-representation from object representations. Mahler (1957), Greenacre (1958), Jacobson (1964), and others have elucidated how different forms of identification play a central role in this transition as maturation makes it possible to progress from total incorporation to selective identifications. The capacity to differentiate between similarities and contrasts eventuates in the capacity to discriminate between inside and outside and ultimately the self and the non-self. In this process, the child learns he is a distinct entity, different from mother, dog, table, etc. However, he also gradually learns by identification to behave and perform certain activities like the mothering person, such as speaking, walking, eating with a spoon, etc. These activities are not duplications, but are modified in accordance with the child's constitution and his mental and physical endowment. The style of his behaviour and activities are further changed by his later identification with others in the environment. What we call identity seems to be the result of the synthesis and integration of different isolated self-representations (Jacobson, 1964; Spiegel, 1959). (61, pp. 371–372)

Finally, Greenson notes:

The boy must attempt to renounce the pleasure and security-giving closeness that identification with the mothering person affords, and he must form an identification with the less accessible father. The outcome will be determined by several elements. The mother must be willing to allow the boy to identify with the father figure.

She can facilitate this by genuinely enjoying and admiring the boy's boyish features and skills and must look forward to his further development along this line (A. Freud, 1965). (61, pp. 372–373)

Perversion

We should not be fooled by those men who do not seem to protect this masculinity, reaching back through it to the earlier identification with mother to create perversion. I think especially of effeminate homosexuals and fetishistic cross-dressers. Although such men want all too much to be like (merge with) their mother—"Perverse rituals serve the function of undoing separation" (1, p. 29)—the rituals serve at the same time, I believe, to promote separation; the essential feature at the bottom of these perversions is that masculinity *is* being preserved. These men, by means of their perversion, retain the potency of their penis, their sense of maleness: that core of masculinity. They have at least some masculinity, to be preserved at any cost. That was why I counted transsexualism not a perversion but more simply a sexual variant. The transsexual never had such an episode of masculinity in his childhood nor can we find such in the adult transsexual, while in effeminate homosexuals, fetishistic cross-dressers, and other men with gender disorders, masculinity is easy to find in their childhood and in the adult. Perhaps perversions are fracture lines resulting from this process of oscillating between desire to merge and desire to separate, and while they may be cemented shut in the nonperverse, covered over in the neurotic, and kept open as channels in the perversions, these faults nonetheless run into the depths of males' identity and require greater reparative work and vigilance than in females. (This is not to say that perversions are simply the product of a disturbance in the separation process undertaken by both mother and infant. I am suggesting, rather, that failure to separate well *can be* a matrix that encourages perversion if events occur later in childhood that require such a detour in sexual development.)

Remember how these ideas fit with conditions in which a male with some masculinity does identify sufficiently with females that he puts on some of their behavior as well as their clothes. To repeat: Such an aberration is a perversion if the femininity (or effeminacy) is determined by an unconsciously remembered, ever-active childhood trauma or frustration with a resultant conflict that must continually be resolved; the resolution is the perversion. The effeminate homosexual values his penis, gets pleasure from it, and is focused on it. He is not feminine (behavior that should be indistinguishable from femininity in a woman) but rather is a caricature of femininity. His identification with women is clouded by hostility. He has good cause for hidden anger: as a child his mother offered him the pleasures of excessive closeness but only when he, because of her bullying, gave up his tendencies toward what his mother considered masculine behavior (144). His masculinity is there, preserved, disguised in the effeminate—*hostile*—mimicry (144).

In transvestism, we also saw masculinity. The usual adult transvestite is a man who, however flawed his gender identity, lives comfortably enough as a masculine person most of the time. He is, however, intermittently propelled into his masquerade of cross-dressing. He does this precisely on behalf of his penis: when excited and in order to have a gratifying penile experience. It is when he disguises his masculinity that he attains the height of maleness, that is, with a potent erection.

The hostility of perversion (and its milder version in the "normal") is a reaction to trauma, a turning outward to find a victim to suit one's revenge. But if one has not felt victimized, then one will not be so motivated. Some confirmation for the thesis comes from those whom I call transsexual. There is in them an odd absence of hostility, a blandness in our relationship, described in more detail elsewhere (147), that persists for years, without end as yet, and unlike what I have ever sensed in any other patients. They treat me as their mothers treated them: as things, as appendages, rather than as separate people. I never have felt in danger from a transsexual, but a painfully large number of my other patients with gender identity disorders have escaped being murderers (of others or of me) only by hard and frightening therapeutic work. One is reported on at book length elsewhere (146).

Discussion

As described here, masculinity in males starts as a movement away from the blissful and dangerous, forever remembered and forever yearned for, mother-infant symbiosis. The male infant who is to become masculine must be blessed with a mother who encourages him to separate from her and to individuate appropriately. If she cannot allow him this, she will prolong and thereby augment his primary state of femininity; and if, on the other hand, she beats at him too harshly to forgo all she considers feminine, she may produce the frozen, brutal, phallic character that results when the possibilities of even momentary return to her are foreclosed (120, 136).

We are certainly familiar with the traumatic effects of anxiety and how it becomes a central factor in motivation. In the case of symbiosis anxiety we have a problem: we must account for an almost universal desire on the part of infants to *separate* themselves from a state of bliss and so to risk anxiety. We can measure the strength of that desire not only by the fact that almost all males develop some degree of masculinity despite the early symbiosis; also, it is known (137) what a monumental effort is required on the part of the transsexual boy's mother to maintain the symbiosis she finds so precious. In accounting for the need to break from mother, some have observed how a mother respectful of maleness and masculinity will reward behavior she considers masculine, discourage that which she does not, time her ministrations to fit the child's mood, capacity, and stage of development, and draw on her husband for necessary reservoirs of masculinity for her son. In addition, perhaps, hatred of mother's badness assists the boy to separate. If, still further, we postulate innate mechanisms pushing the infant toward separation and favoring behavior that can be shaped into what mother feels is masculine, we may have a good enough explanation for the pleasure—the sense of mastery—that will motivate him to remove himself from her.

Once the boy has been acknowledged as a male and has begun to fix that sense of maleness and pride in masculinity into character structure, it becomes crucial that he raise a barrier—symbiosis anxiety—against his tendency to regress into his mother's embrace. Herein, symbiosis anxiety serves an essential normalizing function, permitting the process of disidentifying and then individuation to proceed. Without this barrier, femininity will persist, the oedipal situation will not be perceived as a conflict, the knowledge of mother's body as a separate and desired object (a root of later heterosexuality) will not develop, and masculinity will not be the happy end result.

Perhaps some of the uneasiness men feel about women—the mystery over which poets (male) sentimentalize—reflects the need to raise this barrier against the desire to merge with mother. This, then, could be one more contribution to the multiple causes of homosexuality; lying next to, or even worse, penetrating a woman's body would be too risky. The boy fears losing his masculinity and sense of maleness, not only by losing his

precious, fragile penis but also because he may be over-
whelmed by the desire to become one with the dark
infinity of inner femaleness once again.* This could
partly account for the many men who cannot live lovingly
with a woman except for short periods and for those
who, after intercourse, must get up and away quickly.

Much of this is not new. For instance, in a letter to
Freud dated November 6, 1927, Lou Andreas-Salomé
writes:

> For women have never experienced the great shock of
> discovering the absence of their own penis in their
> mother. In the male it is this discovery which gives rise
> in the first place to the incest-situation, which confirms
> him as a male in relation to the female parent. Thus even
> before the incest-situation has arisen, he has been con-
> fronted with an overwhelming experience, which is to-
> tally suppressed and to which he never returns again in
> later life. Whereas the girl is concerned with real things
> and sensual experience, the man is haunted in the far-
> thest recesses of his mind by a hidden and peculiar
> romanticism, an exciting piece of unreality, which inevi-
> tably continues to exercise a secret influence upon his
> love-life. Whereas, with the help of his castration fears,
> he works through the incest-situation in himself, diverts
> his secret desire from his mother and seeks to degrade
> her, along with her whole sex, more or less to the status
> of a whore, there nevertheless remains in him a primor-
> dial relationship to the "mother figure with a penis," who
> was his sexual equal and yet much superior to himself,
> both protecting and surpassing him. He must find some
> solution to this situation; does he not do so perhaps in
> that love of the "masculine anaclitic type" which you
> have described for us (in *The Ego and the Id*)? This is in
> itself understandable—as a result of the battle against the
> incest, and of the exaggerated reverential tenderness
> which takes its place. If the process is successful, this is

*"The general failure of recognition of absolute dependence at the
start contributes to the fear of WOMAN that is the lot of both men
and women" (155, p. 304).

in part the result of the primordial experience, which seems in this way to re-establish a place for itself in the real world.

Perhaps the fetishist is precisely a person with whom this process has not succeeded, but who then condenses it into an absurd fragment of reality, a boot, a lock of hair or something else, which he then invests with a fantastic splendour. But it is just this absurdity which explains the full significance of the successful libidinal development of the normal person. It has always seemed to me that the male, despite his more conscious and firmer adjustment to reality, nevertheless possessed a spark of a more romantic or "idealistic" or deeply imaginative—or call it what you will—capacity than the female, for which reason he is the more creative. He has resigned more deeply in face of that primordial disappointment and has kept his most imaginative faculties intact untarnished by reality, whence they erupt into creative activity—while the female, despite all sentimental tendencies on her part, never entirely relinquished reality, and so can adopt a sober and harmonious relationship to it. (116, pp. 168–169)

Also, years ago, Boehm, in discussing "the femininity-complex in men" (that is, aspects of masculinity), described the role of fear that arises in boys and men because they envy women's femaleness:

Hatred of women originates in . . . castration anxiety. Because boys imagine that conception and parturition are so complicated and uncanny, and because these processes are so mysterious to them, they have a passionate wish to share in them or else an intense envy of this capacity in women. . . . Envy of the woman's capacity to bear children (which I will call, for short, "parturition-envy") is a considerable incentive to the capacity for production in men.

There is yet another form which men's envy of feminine attributes may assume, namely, envy of the woman's breasts. I think that when we are children we envy others

if they have anything *more* than we ourselves have. It is
inevitable that the female breasts should rouse envy in
boys and call forth the wish to possess these organs,
especially since the breasts, as I mentioned above, represent in the boy's unconscious a tremendous penis. Apart
from this, however, they have a function different from
any possessed by boys. . . .

I said just now that it excites our envy when others
have something *more* than we have ourselves. We may
say, further, that when they have something *different*,
something which we can never have, we experience a
sense of inferiority. The quality of the "different" thing
does not matter very much. We have so often been told,
and every analysis of a woman confirms the fact, that little
girls envy boys their power of passing urine in a continuous stream, further and higher than they themselves can
manage it. But many men can recall an experience of
their nursery days: how their little sisters could pass a
broader stream of urine than they could and how it made
a quite different, duller sound in the chamber. One of my
patients remembered distinctly how it vexed and shamed
him that he could not produce the same noise when
urinating. In later life his great hobby was a garden-hose
from which he could send out either a full stream or a fine
spray of water.

All the phenomena which I have briefly described so
far may be summed up in the term: The femininity-complex in men. (6, pp. 456–457)

One can argue that the transsexual's mother, with her
intense and manifest hatred of males in general, cannot
help but transmit an enraged feeling to her son. Of
course she does transmit that feeling about males in
general, but my observations are that in him she finds an
exception to her rule; he knows that her disparagement
of his father does not include him, the transsexual. This
particular boy—this beautiful phallus—is so much his
mother's prize, the end of her hopelessness, the happy
completion of her formerly inadequate body, the joy of

her life, that there is no reason to expect he will suffer as long as he stays inside the symbiosis. One can *speculate* that he suffers, that anxiety floods through him, that he is psychotic and barely covers it over with the transsexual symptomatology, but that is "explanation" gathering its strength from expectation, not observation. This is not to say that there are not people who use a strong identification with women to defend themselves against such flooding anxiety and who even collapse into psychosis; I see many more such patients than I do transsexuals. But I disagree with those who say such primitive anxiety is also present in these rare cases, the male transsexuals. For that anxiety to appear in the latter people, I would need to believe either, as some Kleinians do, that there is an inherent state of terror in all infants independent of the quality of the mothering (which does not explain why everyone is not a transsexual), or that these mothers are inflicting massive, terrible (though hidden) traumas on their infant sons, sufficient to produce this huge defense but too subtle to be observed.

One *should* suspect that hostility directed upon him by his mother would help cause the transsexual's femininity; it does so in effeminate homosexuals and transvestites (3, 144). Since she expresses her hatred and envy of other males, it is not likely this mother can restrain herself with her son, no matter how she might consciously try. While that is likely (and was the position I assumed years ago when first studying the symbiosis), the hostility just has not appeared. That can be due to its subtlety, my ineptness, or its absence, and I have struggled over these possibilities.

At present, I can still only say that I have not found that hostility inside the symbiosis. If nonetheless it is there, it should eventually make its presence known. Gender reversal is a massive shift in identity; it is not likely to be caused by some puny whisper of mother's will. If hatred or its permutations are strong, the effects should also be reflected in the infant in forms with which those studying children have long since familiarized us: defective nongender ego development, such as delay or precocity in intellectual functions, motility, or speech; disorders in physiological functions such as sleep, feeding, muscle turgor, and crying; out-of phase, unintegrated development; disruptive affects such as rage, terror, depression, apathy, anxiety, withdrawal—inappropriate, excessive, bizarre, or ill-timed; distorted or delayed development of object relations—with family or strangers, humans or animals, animate or inanimate objects; reduced or absent curiosity; reduced or absent creativity, as in games or fantasying; thought disorders in nongender areas; and so forth. Almost never is even one of these effects present in any of the little boys I call transsexuals.

By no means is this blissful merging to be confused with the "fusion, meeting, and lack of differentiation between the self and nonself" (90, p. 309) noted in children who are the product of psychotic symbiosis. Transsexuals' mothers hold their babies too long and too close, but they do not restrict motility (that would be another sign of maternal hostility), which might discourage finding the nonself world. These mothers help their sons define the borders between self and outside world in all regards except mother's femaleness and femininity. They also encourage the boys' creativity and the growth of other ego functions, so that these boys are typically lively, alert, and artistic (60, 137)—again suggesting that mother's hostility is weak or absent in the symbiosis.

As the boys grow, they are not isolates but, instead, easily fit in with peers in games and studies. Only as they enter the phase of unmerciful harassment, in school, for being feminine do they turn away from others.

This explanation may be unpalatable, for it suggests that a major deviation in character structure can be created atraumatically. Yet atraumatic pressures are among the most important factors in the development of character structure, both "normal" and "abnormal."

This chapter is about masculinity in males. Yet the thesis about the role of the early symbiosis ought to be tested with females as well: is femininity augmented, as the thesis would predict, in a wholesome mother–female infant symbiosis, and is masculinity in females encouraged by lessening intimacy in the symbiosis? There are hints of confirmation: the most masculine females known, the female transsexuals, seem to develop out of the following: they are not considered beautiful or graceful at birth; they are not cuddly infants; there is a markedly flawed symbiosis, with their mother not psychologically or physically available in the first months or more of life and no adequate person to substitute; the girl is encouraged, especially by her father, to be strong and masculine, that is, not to need symbiosis (141). (Recall also the relationship of the transsexual boy's mother to her mother for a related inadequate symbiosis that contributes to her masculinity.) These factors suggest that, as with males, foreshortening the symbiosis and making its attenuation worthwhile creates in females those behaviors and that identity we designate as masculinity. (One aspect of the next book reporting on my research will be the development of femininity in girls and women.)

Let me summarize. Mothers, we see, have an additional task in rearing a son not needed with a daughter. They must encourage the separation (1) with greater intensity, steadfastness, and vigilance; (2) at the right time(s); (3) with the right amounts of frustration tempered with (4) the right amounts of love, care, and sympathy; (5) enjoying their husband enough to offer this father as a worthy object for identification.

In addition to encouraging the separation, they must also encourage the development of a sense of mastery. This has been studied in regard to many ego functions

but perhaps less systematically in regard to those functions that are perceived by others and by oneself as masculinity. It requires of a mother (1) that her own envy of
maleness be subdued; (2) that she be feminine, or, if not
particularly so, that she be so in certain regards at least
when with her sons (146); and (3) that she enjoy infants.
It is a great advantage (4) if she is genuinely heterosexual
and especially helpful if she is married, so that a loved
masculine man can be permanently present in the
family.*

In biology—of animals and man—maleness is a quality
that differentiates out of a female anlage. Analogously,
as hypothesized here, masculinity is a quality that differentiates out of a feminine anlage. To convert this hypothesis to a finding will require that we bring a clinical
"microscope" to bear on the mother-infant relation-
ship† to examine the manner in which the symbiosis
dissolves into two people who know each other's differences. This act of dissolution will bring the infant boy to
the world and to his masculinity.

Here is a proposition that can in time be tested empiri-
cally: our culture, as do most others, defines masculinity
—for better or worse—by how completely one demonstrates that one is rid of the need for symbiosis with
mother.

*These feminine qualities are summed up, in their absence, in
McDougall's comment: "In the child destined to a perverse solution
of sexual desire the mother's unconscious plays a vital role. One is
tempted to surmise that the mother of the future pervert herself
denies sexual reality and denigrates the father's phallic function. It is
possible that she gives the child in addition the feeling that he or she
is a phallic substitute" (103, p. 381).
†We can expect to do so because of—more than anyone else—
Mahler. She has pointed the way, with her methodology and her
conceptualizations, to our being able to focus precisely on the dynamics in mother-infant relationships.

Chapter 9

A Crime as
a Sexual Act

In this chapter is information that complicates the concept of perversion. The criminal act to be studied is a habitual piece of behavior that falls somewhere between a perversion—an erotic neurosis—and a neurosis whose symptoms are not overtly erotic. For this patient the overt sexual act—arranging a "rape"—is devoid of erotic pleasure, while a nonerotic part of her ritual—breaking into a house—almost literally simulates intercourse without the patient's conscious awareness, rather like the hysterical convulsions of Victorian days. Her perversion thus illustrates Freud's point that neurotic and psychotic symptoms are (I would say, *may be*) disguised, unconscious sexual activity.* This case is presented also to make visible the form of primitive sexual impulses that have been unconscious until made manifest.

The patient, who has been reported on extensively elsewhere (146), is a woman in her thirties who, until

---

*I do not, however, believe as Schmideberg does "that most acts of pathological delinquency can be classed wholly or partly as perversions or fetiches" (124, p. 45), an odd opinion that she holds simply because both are "repetitive acts" with "a clearly marked and rigid pattern" (p. 45). That is hardly a sufficient reason to equate the two. Would she call all rituals sexual perversions?

treatment (not analysis) ended, was usually extremely masculine, was intermittently psychotic with hallucinations and delusions, and suffered from trance states and multiple personality. She also was firmly convinced that she possessed a penis of the same anatomical dimensions and quality as a normal male's, though positioned inside her pelvis. The most important part of treatment for her was her search to find her self, an insoluble task till then because she had times when she clearly felt herself to be the female she wanted to be and at other times just as clearly experienced herself as the male she wanted to be —and sometimes when she wanted to feel like a female, she felt like a male instead; and vice versa.

In her teens and early twenties, she had indulged in numerous forms of criminal behavior—from bad-check writing to attempted murder—for which she was at times arrested and imprisoned. In the following material, from several years ago and after many years of treatment, she reveals for the first time the ritual (the *modus operandi*, the M.O. that the police know fits many criminals like a fingerprint) she used when breaking into homes for the purpose of robbery. While reading this material, the reader may think of kleptomania, with its known dynamics that relate to a woman's desire to steal a penis (19, pp. 370–371), a penis that fills one up as only a feeding breast can. However, this patient's experience is not quite that of a kleptomaniac, if only because the dynamics are so poorly disguised as compared with those of the average kleptomaniac. This woman's criminal act is like perversion in being repetitive, gratifying, driven, built from dynamics of hostility, and in converting a victim into a victor. The difference is that it is not erotic, even though the genitals are the arena, and though one step in the ritual demands intercourse and another is an act in which the body is used as a genital.

Finally, because a crime is committed as part of this complicated sexual ritual, we are thrown into moral questions that, since they concern responsibility for one's actions, can serve as a bridge to the problem of sin touched on in the last section of this book.

At one point, the transcript reveals the patient slipping from a state of full consciousness into a trance. By this stage, toward the end of treatment, she was able to go into trance at will, an aspect of her capacity to split her self into parts; other aspects of this capacity are her multiple personalities and hallucinatory states. During these trances, she would relive—not just remember—experiences from the past, including events in earliest childhood that she was unable to recall when fully conscious.

In this discussion the patient and I are quite free with each other, trusting, without politeness, tact, or social grace. Most of my extended, explanatory remarks—we both know—are half questions and half probes to stimulate further my, as well as her, understanding; they are not—as they may seem in print—a drumfire of positively stated interpretations. Despite the risks, the case material is presented here by means of the words the patient and I spoke to each other. I have chosen this method in order to let the reader glimpse in what way theory arises from data in my research. There is a great distance between what was said in the treatment (or at least the pallid ghost that remains when talk is printed) and the theory and hypotheses with which this book is loaded. And one should wonder: (when) should any theory in a scientific endeavor be taken seriously if the data behind it are, as in psychoanalysis, not available?

S. Why do you want to do it?

G. Because it gives me something. You don't know how neat it is . . . It's better than sex . . . to go some place and get in and steal. It's better than getting a woman. When I first started to steal, when I was a little kid, I stole food, yeah. I can remember going into . . . they had victory gardens when I was a kid and I remember stealing food . . . I don't remember it being terribly exciting; I remember it being satisfying because my belly was empty. When I was about thirteen: screw them up; see how bad you can screw 'em up and the more you can steal . . . I don't even know what I did with what I . . . I probably gave it away; that's what I do with most things I steal; I give them away. I don't want them. When I was in junior high school, we used to go in groups. One would act as a lookout, one would be a cover, and I was always the one who would steal. I chose it. I not only chose it for myself, they chose it for me because I was so capable. I'm scared every time I steal. I'm not scared of getting caught. I don't know what I'm scared of.

After it's over, I'm so excited . . . I am so excited. I don't shake or anything while I'm doing it. I don't . . . no big stuff. When I'm done, I shake until my hands shake; I shake all over. I walk around the block, I fuck somebody, usually I eat. I always eat a hot fudge sundae. I don't know why. Because that's what appeals to me. . . . Do you know there's a restaurant, when they see me come in they make a huge hot fudge sundae in a soup bowl? I only go in there for a hot fudge sundae. They don't know me; I'm a stranger to them. I go there every time, afterwards.

Another unvarying part of her M.O. was to seek out a strange man, a machine chosen because he looked capable of forceful, unfeeling, frozen, unloving intercourse with a rigid penis, a sexual act that she could not have borne, much less would have sought, at any other time.

G. I just lay there and get fucked. [To her this word never means only intercourse; it is used here for its precise evocation of forced attack on a female.] They [men] can do anything to me they want to. I don't even know if I come. [At no other time does she not know.] I'm not talking about sex; I'm talking about

getting fucked. It's just important to get fucked
. . . like being ripped open. If the first man can't do
that, I go out and get another one. It depends on how
lucky I am. If I do get the right one the first time, then
that's all. If not, I go for one after the other till I feel
like I've been fucked. I tell him to fuck me. That's
what I want. If I have an orgasm, it's not in my genitals; it's in my head. An explosion. And then I'm
relieved; I'm not shaking any more.

I'd do this at least once a month; at least. At most
once a week. I've never stolen without doing all this.
It was starting by the time I was in my teens, when
the boys—my friends—and I stole some cars and
went to Arizona [age fourteen]. I stole them. Then I
got fucked. On the way to Arizona. That night. We
were in Arizona the next morning.

The night after she described this to me, the feeling—
a craving—to steal, to eat ice cream, and to be raped
returned.

During her next treatment hour, she filled in more of
the ritual.

S. What did you used to do with the stuff you'd steal?
G. It depends on what it was. Most of it I gave away. Just
about anything of value except . . . not appliances,
nothing big, the big stuff that would be difficult to
carry out. It depends too . . . well, if I was doing it
for myself, I'd steal small things. If I'm stealing because I wanted to satisfy something in myself, I'd
steal only one object. If I'm stealing for my partner,
I'd steal something else. I almost never kept anything. One time I kept a music box for a long, long
time.

There follows a discussion of techniques and knowledge that reveals the patient's professionalism. As she
talks, she becomes ashamed.

G. I didn't go out last night [despite the return of the impulse].

I dreamt about when I was a kid and we didn't have a refrigerator; we had an icebox, and the iceman came and I could remember him saying that too. I don't know why I dreamt it, but I can remember saying it . . . When we were kids, when the man would deliver the ice, we would crawl in the back of the truck while he was in the house, and I dreamt about that last night, about him being in the house and I climbed in the back of the truck to get some ice and he came out and told me that if I stole his ice, he was going to stab me with his ice pick. And I thought that would really be neat, to be stabbed with an ice pick.* I wasn't scared.

I'm not evil when I steal. I don't steal because I'm evil. I steal because I need to and it's not because I'm bad. If I were to sit and think: I'm going to steal from this little old lady in Pasadena and this is her life's savings and her family heirlooms and all that then I suppose I would feel evil, but I couldn't do that. I don't steal from anybody. I don't think about anybody. They just don't exist . . . I'm not evil, because I'm not doing it to hurt anybody . . . I want to cry but I won't. I don't know . . . because I feel like I'm a little kid that's being punished for something I didn't do. Maybe if I were punished, I wouldn't do it any more.

I'll tell you what just came in my mind. Starting with the doctor and him saying, "Why do you have to have a baby?" [She had repeatedly had illegitimate babies] and me saying, "Well, you know, when something's gone, you have to have something to replace it." When it's taken away from you, you've got to have it back or you feel empty inside. The stealing takes a couple of days to build up. I first notice it

---

*As a child, she had once, in a rage, stabbed her mother in the thigh; that was as high as she could reach.

when I wake up. Hungry. In my stomach. I don't eat; it's not that kind of hungry. I used to eat, and I would throw up. I would have the feeling . . . I was thinking about this old man . . . When I was a kid, maybe eight, there was this old man that I used to go and visit. He lived in a cellar. His son and daughter-in-law and her kids lived upstairs and he had an apartment downstairs, and he would tell me, "You can only have that [a gift he had for her] if you steal it. I'm not going to give it to you, but if you steal it, you can have it." And one day my sister and I went to see him and he was dead . . . It really wasn't stealing, then.

That morning when it starts, I'd wake up; I always wake up early, you know, when it's still dark, and something wakes me up and I'm hungry. Maybe it's a bad thought in my sleep or something. But I don't remember. But I'm excited. I don't want to get out of bed. I'm . . . something. I don't want to get out of bed . . .

I always dress the same. I always do the same things. I've worn the same clothes. But I always wore the same style clothes. A pair of Levis and tennis shoes and a shirt.

S. What kind of shirt?

G. Just a shirt. It's not a woman's shirt . . . A man's shirt. My own. It's mine.

S. What kind?

G. It's a solid color. Long sleeves.

S. Always?

G. Yes, but I roll them up to here. Blue. I like blue shirts. I don't know why. Always a blue shirt. I know it couldn't be red or green.

S. Who, if anyone, rolled up their sleeves and wore blue shirts?

G. I don't know . . . My grandfather did.

S. And why are the sleeves rolled up?

G. Because it's more comfortable that way.

S. Then why not wear a short-sleeve shirt?

G. Because it's too short.

S. Look, you do think it's evil. The fucking seems to be a punishment: you can't have any of this [goodness] until you've had that [punishment]. Once you've been properly punished then your conscience lets you have the whole thing. Which is: peace. And it's something about the iceman.

G. The iceman wore a leather thing over his shoulder so when he . . .

S. Who was he?

G. It's time to go . . . [I do not let her.] We had an iceman and a bakery man and a milkman, and they all disliked my mother. The bakery man used to pad her bill and then give me the money. We didn't always have an iceman. It was just when I was very young . . . I don't know . . . I don't know.

S. Is your father in any of this?

G. No.

S. Has he got any [qualities] of the blue shirt, the rolled-up sleeves, or the iceman?

G. Do you know, when you asked me about the blue shirt . . . I had a picture of my father coming home, with his sleeves rolled up and his sweater, he had a sweater, I remember it very distinctly, and he always hung it on the doorknob and there would be something in the pocket for me. Something just for me. It was a strange thing that he did, because I had brothers and sisters, you know. I had to sneak to get it so the other kids wouldn't see it. Because he only brought it to me; he didn't bring anything to the other kids.

S. So you stole it!

G. Yeah. And the thing I steal, it's for me. First I hold it in my hand and then take it home.

S. And then you have the ice cream: you celebrate. And then you get fucked, the big punishment. Now, what did your mother do about this little game?

G. She was always angry because he never brought any-thing to the others . . .

S. Your daddy never put you into a shirt like that, did he?

G. He used to put me into his clothes. A shirt and pants, the whole works. He thought it was very funny to dress me up in his clothes.

S. Did he roll your sleeves up?

P. Sure, they were too long.

Then comes material about her mother that would be too difficult for the reader to follow because the associa-tions and interpretations refer to events and ideas from the years of treatment that have preceded this moment. Suffice to say that in an hour shortly before the iceman dream, she had said her mother had ice in her veins, and so the hour just described ended with my suggesting the iceman was Mrs. G.'s frozen, unyielding mother who represented death to her in her infancy and childhood. (One can get a fuller picture of her relationship with her mother in [146].)

Next hour.

G. The thing I take is only valuable to me for a cer-tain length of time, and then I have to get rid of it. The only thing that I stole that I kept for any length of time was a music box. It was a child's music box. It had little carved figures on it. It was like a merry-go-round, and it had children that went around in a circle when the music played . . . I never stole anything "valuable" unless I was stealing for my partner. Say there was a piece of jewelry on the table and there was a rock, I might more likely take the rock than the jewelry . . . I keep them a couple of days and then give them away. Throw them away—anything. The things I take are not trivial, but you're going to think they're trivial. When I go into a house, I look around; I don't know what the value is of things, but if they look to me to be of *that* kind of value, then I take them. Not monetary value.

S. Why do you get rid of them? Why don't they stay valuable?

G. For the same reason I throw out the garbage; all the value is out of them. I don't need them. Now I have the feeling inside, the feeling that I get from taking the object.

Next hour. Between this one and the previous, the patient sent me a letter and phoned. She now refers to these communications.

G. This [the subject of stealing] doesn't have anything to do with me being a baby.

S. Of course not. You write me a letter about breasts and dreams of breasts and you tell me that you drink . . . what is it, a half a gallon of milk a day . . . and in the last day or so you've been eating like an absolute pig. And last night, twice, deliciously, you wet yourself.

G. I was thinking about when my mother called last night.

S. [She has reported to me on the phone]: You fell asleep early in the evening and you wet the bed. You awoke from it feeling, "Oh, isn't that great." And then she called while you were still in bed?

G. Yes. I almost remembered something, and just now I thought, "God, now I remember," but I don't know what it is. [In retrospect, I realize this was the first move toward a trance; usually such almost remembering is not related to a trance.]

What I see in my head is my mother breastfeeding a baby. I don't know which one [of G.'s younger siblings]. I feel hungry. My mother always smelled good. Something warm and good. Probably if it hadn't been so cold . . . When my grandmother held me, you know, my grandmother was fat and had big breasts, soft, you could just kind of sink in; that wasn't the same as my mother. I don't know. I just don't want to . . . I just don't want to think about bad things. [Slides into light trance.]

Remember about the . . . do you remember putting the baby nipple to make it look like a penis? [She had done this as a child because she wanted a penis badly.] "That doesn't go there—it goes in your mouth." [She seems here to be quoting her mother's remark.] But you can't have both, you know, you have to decide which is more important [the nipple in the mouth or the penis on the body]. I don't know any more which is more important. The way it was then, everything . . . everything goes in the mouth, everything. None of it is ever right though. You know, when you put your thumb in your mouth . . . there's a hole there, there's an empty spot there. Because the hole never fills up. And that makes this hurt right here [lips]. It makes it tight, frustrated.

S. Now tell me about when you get enough.

G. When you have that thing [the stolen object] in your hand . . .

D. Do you put it in your mouth?

G. Yeah. I put it against my mouth. It's cool. I don't have to cry. It just feels good. . . . Don't you remember those things? [In trance.] There was little ducks, you know. It's very hard to get it into my mouth.

S. What's the best thing?

G. My mother. It smells good. When she put me in the bathtub, you know, when we were both in the bathtub, I stole it.

I don't remember . . . I'm tired . . . I don't know . . . It was the only time I was warm . . . I don't want to cry . . . Let's go to another place . . . I need to go somewhere else. You have to know what goes where. If you're a boy . . . I don't know what to do when I'm a boy. I don't know what to do. I don't remember how to do that. Do you know, I tried very hard—I just could never do it right. I need to go somewhere else. Do you want to go? Why are you always here? You're always here. There are so many terrible places there. Can you hear that? [Hallucination in trance; experiences self now as a child.] If I was tall enough . . . I just don't understand. I don't know how they can expect those kinds of things. You know, they tell me so many different kinds of things. First they say that's O.K. and then they smack me, and I never know what I'm supposed to do. And that boy, he just . . . he's just so bad. Do you know, it wouldn't be so bad if it wasn't always cold.

S. It isn't always cold. Isn't it warm when you wet?

G. Yeah.

S. Isn't that why you wet?

G. Yeah. That's almost as good as being in the bathtub with somebody that's good. You know, one time I was there and I was cold and it just came to me [to wet] and it felt so good. You remember when I was in a cage [a cagelike box used as a crib during her first year of life], I did it when I was awake. There's two good things: being warm and having your mouth full . . . if you have it with her.

S. When you were wet, what did you do to make your mouth full?

G. I put my thumb in my mouth or the good things. Like the duck. The blanket; but there's only a part of the blanket you can put in your mouth. Where the ribbon is. When I have my own children, I put them in my mouth. My friends, too. You know, not men, except maybe their chest or something. Or bite; I want to bite. I put all of women in my mouth. But if you do that, you're going to get hurt.

Do you feel that? [A sensation inside her; touches her abdomen.] It was just a little excitement to get something. The feeling is right here [lips] that goes right here [stomach] . . . Last night it was the need to be warm and wet. I remember, I remember how good it felt.

S. You talked to me on the phone last night. I told you not to go out in the street [to obey the impulse to steal]. I told you that something else would take its place. And you wet. Why did you do it when you were asleep?

G. I couldn't do that when I'm awake. . . . I was dreaming about being in the bathtub. I dreamt that I was wet and warm. If you pee on yourself, you get spanked. I remembered both things last night. That it feels good and it feels bad.

I dreamt about the woman with the breasts. You know, going there and taking them. I'm not going there . . . we just went to . . . to that place, the hot springs that was warm and it smelled good; that's wrong, because it never smells good there, but it did smell good there, and she was there taking a bath and I just came up behind her but she wasn't angry. I took her breasts. I just took them in my hands and put them in my mouth. And then I was wet. I was wet and warm.

[Out of trance.] I'm getting very tired. I'm tired of many things. I'm tired of doing the wrong thing; I'm tired of the bad feelings; I'm tired of those kind of thoughts that come in my sleep . . . Of wanting those things that I shouldn't have. I'm tired of not remembering what's the right things, you know . . . Nobody should cry. If you cry, you're going to get something to cry for.

S. Is that what you believe or is that what she says?

G. I don't know. I'm not going to find out.

Next hour.

S. O.K. How is the eating? Has it stopped?

G. What eating?

S. And the craving has gone?

G. Yeah. I feel pretty good today. I feel pretty good. And I bought myself a duck, a real neat duck. [I had given the patient a few dollars with the instruction not to use it for food and clothes but to buy something for herself because she had never done that in the past. When she was a child, the family had been bone poor and her mother frozen, too much to permit a few pennies to be spent for "something good." In recent years, the patient had never stolen things of value that she had kept for herself. And so she was deeply in debt. Even had she had money—and at times, she had the dollars in her hand and could have impulsively indulged—"it never occurred to me to buy something good."]

S. Is that something you've never done in the past? Yes, you never have?

G. Yes, I never have. I was just thinking about . . . I'm going tonight to dinner at D.'s [a friend's] house, and I was thinking: I wonder if that top shelf really gets dusty and my ducks are up there, and I was thinking about my ducks. I have quite a few ducks. People say, "What do you want?" and I'll say, "Give me a duck." I have some ducks from when I was . . . I have a rubber duck that I've had since I was an infant.

S. Is that the one that you were thinking of yesterday?

G. I don't know; I don't know what you're talking about.

S. You talked about when you were an infant having a duck and rubbing it against your mouth.

G. I don't know. I don't remember that.

   Wait a minute. We should be talking about . . . something. I really don't think the whole thing is breasts. It doesn't feel comfortable to me. I have feelings about breasts, you know; I dig breasts, you know [chuckles]. The thing that puzzles me the most is: why steal? Why that particular method of getting something? Why not buy something? Then there's the part about getting in [into a house]. And when I say getting in, I think about getting into this and getting into that, like . . . I'm thinking about getting into a woman or . . . and what flashes through my head is my son being born or my daughter being born and my saying, "Put her back." All those things are going through my head. Yesterday when I went to the store to buy the duck, there was a woman coming out of the store as I was going in, and I just pushed through very . . . very impolitely . . . it just felt good to get in. Do you know what I mean? I have never stolen from stores, only homes. But to satisfy the impulse, it could only be a private home in which a family lives; dark and quiet. And not cold. And not a place that was easy to get into. I can get into any apartment building in my area. I've broken into my own apartment dozens of times when I've forgotten my key. It's very simple to get into an apartment. It would never occur to me to go into one of *those* places and steal anything. (You know, you've making me nervous—that's what you're really doing.) An apartment is not a home. Most apartments are where just a woman lives or a man lives or . . . In a home there's a mother and a father and children.

You know that even after I was taken out of the box [see above] I used to crawl in it. I just thought of it. I just see myself crawling in the box. That's where my blanket was, anyway. It was hard to get in. It was a big box. I had to tip it over . . . I think that's why I felt so comfortable about being in jail. When I bust into a house, it's always dark. That's not for safety; I just never have the desire to do it at, say, two o'clock in the afternoon. It's good if it's cold outside. I always feel like I've been there before, like I know where I am, and it's good to be getting there where it's comfortable. It's not a good idea to go up to the door. And then there are things you have to do for your own safety . . . like, you can get your leg bitten off by a dog. So I'd make sure there's no dog. It's really neat to go in through a window. Windows are hard to open except the kind they're putting in houses now—they're easy . . . I don't want to do this [that is, tell about the ritual].

I want to squeeze in. It's nice if there's curtains on the window. To brush against. I suppose I get in the smallest place I can. If not, why don't I go through a sliding glass door or something which is relatively easy to open? Before . . . I'm tense. I don't know exactly. It's like you're all worked up for something, anxious to . . . like if you were having sex and you were right up there and ready . . . And then when I get in, it's good. It's . . . it's warm in there; it's . . . it's a giving place to be. Does that make sense? And I can go whewwwww, it's so neat. And then when I've got it in the hand, when I've got it in my hand, then I can leave, it's all done; it's all finished. Then it doesn't make any difference how I leave; I can go by the front door. I don't have to crawl out. And then . . . and then the bad part . . . it's not really bad, you would think it was bad maybe. I don't know what you think; some people would think it was bad. And that's the part about getting fucked. That's really necessary; you really have to be punished for doing that; it [breaking in] was really a bad thing to do. But it never makes it go away, you know; it doesn't make any difference how bad you get fucked, it just comes back. The getting fucked does *not* make it go away. But getting the *thing* makes it go away, makes the hunger part go away. Sometimes I think when I'm wandering around the street or doing whatever I'm doing: looking for a place to get into that . . . this isn't going to make any sense but I think . . . I don't think I'm a woman. Do you know what I mean? I don't think I'm a female. No, it's . . . I really will be . . . really a functional, complete, thinking, feeling, wanting, male individual. It is some different from when I'd feel I was a female but I still knew I had a penis. When I was little and thought, "Well, I'll be a good boy," I always knew I was a girl; I knew that, you know. Or when I had a penis, all I had to do was spread my legs and there I was a female, you know, but when I'm walking [toward a break-in] and I have my male's clothes on . . .

S. Do you have a penis?

G. I don't know. I don't know if I've got a tongue.

S. That's what I mean: it doesn't have anything to do with the penis.

G. No. No, no, no.

S. It's different from the whole penis thing. It's got nothing to do with anatomy or with the clothes you were wearing.

G. Right. What else would I wear if I was a man? The clothes are immaterial . . . After we talked yesterday . . . yesterday I didn't feel like a man [any longer]. I didn't feel like anything. I felt *good,* you know; I didn't think about am I a man or a woman or what have I got on or . . . I wonder how that happened? *That's* the strange thing.

S. Has it happened before?

G. No.

S. The first time in your life?

G. Yes.

S. And all because I gave you money and told you to buy something good. What was it like, yesterday?

G. Yesterday it was ishooohhhhh, wow! "Wow, I can go out; I know who I am and I'm walking with my sister and my sister knows who am I"; and the man in the store that sold me the duck said, "Thank you, ma'am" . . . You knew who I was and you gave me . . . you gave *me* the money to spend because you know who I am. And when I came here with my sister [later in the day, for a social visit] with the duck, I wanted to put my arms around you and hug you and say, "Oh, thank you." And I did say, "Thank you."

S. Now how much beyond what you get when you steal is that feeling?

G. There's no comparison. When I get that thing in my hand, you know, I still . . . I have to think about the whole thing. I know what I am when I'm going into the house—it's obvious, you know—I'm just a man getting in. But there's something about being a man that I know is wrong, you know—I haven't got the words to tell you, I can't . . . I just want to be warm and . . . I want somebody to know who I am . . . What do I want to be? I don't think I want to be a man. You looked at me yesterday, and you knew who I was. I can be out there on the street and look at myself and not know who I am . . . How do I know who I am—nobody else knows? Nobody ever told me who I was. I need to be somebody definite . . . you know. Yesterday I was real to you. When I've broken in and I have the thing in hand, I feel good about myself, but there's something bad . . . it's like, I don't have a right to be what I am at that time; I have to be punished for what I am at that particular time. But I can never really be "me" until I can have it without stealing. But yesterday, you said, "I'm going to give it to *you.* I'm *giving* to *you*—it's not a loan or anything . . ."

She has given us some idea of why she steals. As an infant, she craved closeness to her frozen mother, from whom she could extract almost no milk or warmth; and she yearned to be part of an intact, loving family. In parts of the ritual we can see her working out her scenario, built, on an oral level, out of risk, mystery, and reversal of victim into victor quite as the erotic story is for excitement on a genital level.

In keeping with the proposition that all the elements

in such story lines could be accounted for if we knew enough, let us turn next to the hour following the one above. The subject is her maleness, a quality invented to assuage her devastating vulnerability. Unwanted by her mother when born, as she grew she saw how her brother —a few years older—was admired; she decided it was maleness that made her mother desire her brother and freeze her out. So from age four on she had a penis; it signified maleness: strength and power to prevent her from feeling cold, starved, abandoned, and humiliated. (See [146] for more about her penis.) But delusion was not enough, nor even the use of women's bodies, especially breasts, to quiet hunger. She also needed a piece of reality she could literally hold in her hand and rub on or put in her mouth. Stealing the gratifying objects provided the comfort for a moment, and in stealing them she revenged herself in fantasy on her ungiving mother.

But this bad act demanded punishment (or rather, as in all masochistic acts, only that punishment one chooses for oneself; no matter how painful in reality, it is at bottom a controlled, partial, gratifying, libidinized—fake— punishment). To satisfy her immense guilt for stealing what her mother (by now the world) would not give her freely, she briefly renounced her penis: in undefended femaleness, she arranged with equanimity her "rape"— penis, and invulnerability, returning only when that was completed.

We can see the form her maleness takes in the ritual of breaking in. It needs little imagination to know she senses herself as a penis thrusting into a woman's body —her mother—a return to primordial bliss. This symbolism approximates that of perverse acts, yet the purpose —and result—is not erotic pleasure; and to call it a perversion blurs the meaning of that word.

S. At what point do you first sense that you're a man?
G. In walking up to the house, I guess. I have to be

walking. I don't feel like a man when I'm in a car. Why wouldn't I feel like that in my car? I guess it's because it's my car.

S. You mean: when you get out of the car, you have disconnected from yourself as a female—physically disconnected. But you dressed in advance appropriately for what's going to happen. You've got on a man's shirt, a man's pants, tennis shoes [for silence and safe footing]—clothes which used to be exclusively men's clothes when you were a kid. What kind of underwear do you have on? [Patient looks stunned.] You forgot about that.

G. Yeah. I don't even know if I wear underwear. I must wear underwear. I guess I just wear my regular underwear, my bra and my pants . . . That "man" has a bra and pants on!

S. O.K. You're out of the car and you're a man and you're looking over the neighborhood for the right house. How do you choose?

G. It's got to be a home. It's got a mother and a father and children. You can tell because maybe they have a bicycle in the yard . . .

S. The person then who climbs through the window is the man?

G. Uh-huh . . . No; I'm not sure. I can think about going up to the house and I can think about having it in my hand . . . it must be . . . it has to be . . . It has to be a man that goes through the window. Who else would go into that kind of an opening? It's just that kind of opening for a man, you know.

S. How do you go through it? Show me your body going through.

G. No. It's too embarrassing . . . I go in head first. Just pull my body in. I do the same thing each time. I go in head first. I pull myself in with my arms, with my hands. I don't know how. Don't ask me. I could just as well go in feet first; it would be more easy sometimes. But it's always head first. You can't go in too fast; you might make some noise . . . I don't want to talk to you any more.

S. When you go in the window, are you fat or thin? [In reality she was fat.]

G. I'm my real self. Thin . . . When I go through the window, I'm on my stomach. My legs are hanging straightly. I guess like this. [Her feet, ankles, and legs are touching; the arms are stiffly, fully extended on a straight line with her rigid body and head.] Like a polliwog. One piece. It wouldn't be curves or it wouldn't be sharp angles. If I was a thing, I would say: I would go in as straight as an arrow. I'm warm and I'm real and I'm that thing that is real . . . you know. I'm a man that's real. Yet you'd be confused. There would be something wrong. See, it's dark and there I am with short hair and pants on, but I have that thing in my hand. So how are you going to know if I'm a boy or a girl? *You have to know.* How am I going to know if *you* don't know?

S. Is that missing every time you're in the house, that somebody hasn't told you?

G. What do you think I have to get fucked for? [Her overriding hope in treatment was that she might someday fully restore her sense of femaleness and accept herself wholly as a woman. "Getting fucked" served to force her to full awareness that her body was female.]

S. I don't know. You're telling me. O.K. I thought it was only to punish you. What about the ice cream?

G. It's all the same thing.

S. O.K. I'm understanding better. When you drop in the window, once your whole body, even your toes have passed through, that's the end of being a man. And once you are walking, you are what . . . uncertain? . . . until you get fucked.

G. Then it's all kinds of things, you know. The fucking

is for being bad and for being what I am and for not
being what I am . . .

S. I want to go back. You have dropped in. What are
you then? You're not sure. You pick up the thing. Do
you get a little bit more sure, or does it stay the same?

G. Yeah, then, see, I . . . if you saw me, you'd be confused. I don't know.

S. But do I get less confused or do I stay equally confused from the minute you drop in until you get
fucked? Isn't there a changing in the degree of confusion? Don't you get more like a woman as the time
goes on?

G. Yeah.

S. When you walk into the ice cream . . .

G. But see, that's not really fair.

S. Why?

G. Because I don't know if that's what I'm supposed to
be: a woman.

S. Do you do it to become a woman?

G. Sure.

S. The craving is partly to become a woman when you
want to steal?

G. To know . . . what I'm supposed to know about
. . . See, when I have it in my hand, I almost remember . . . I can't remember. I've tried so hard. I feel it
in my breasts and in my—everything. Did you . . .
when you were a kid did you ever go and catch pol-
liwogs and keep them in a jar and then they got legs?
A polliwog looks like I do. That's what I really was,
I was a polliwog. Before I lost my tail. When I was
four and a half months old I was already too old, I
was too old to keep on being whatever I was; it was
too late then.

S. You've left something out. When you slide in the
window, what happens immediately after you're in?
What do you feel in your body?

G. It's really very confusing . . . If I didn't wear the
underwear, I wouldn't be a woman when I had it in

my hand. I don't have any breasts when I go through the window. How can a man have breasts?

S. What happens to those things on your chest which are inside your brassiere as you go over the window-sill, whether you tell yourself they're there or not? What happens to them? How do you keep from knowing they're there?*

G. It isn't a matter of knowing they're there. Men don't have breasts. I guess by not touching them or . . . I guess I just ignore [disavowal? splitting? suppression? repression? What is the subjective experience these technical terms cannot quite capture?] them. I don't remember knowing they're there. It's just not logical to have breasts when you're a man. Why do you have to do anything if you know they're not there?

S. Do you know what you are when you go through the window? What does it feel like?

G. It's like getting into a warm, tight place.

S. When you go through the window, are you a man or are you a thing?

G. I was a man when I started to go in the window. I must be a thing, because I'm not anybody. Then it feels strong and good and . . . I really do want to just be me. Do you know . . . when I was a patient here on the ward and they'd say, "You look confused" or "You sound confused" or I would say, "Oh, well, I'm confused about this"—that was all so irrelevant: *there is no confusion like the confusion about not knowing whether you're real or not or what you are or . . .* [My italics; she spoke softly.]

S. Let me go back for a moment. When you go out and wear a woman's underwear, what do you do about that when you turn into a man?

G. The same thing I do with my breasts. But there must

*I am trying here to comprehend the moment—the state of consciousness, the yearning for regression—when hysterical conversion occurs.

be a part of me that knows it, because I know when I get in that house I *need* that underwear and I *need* those breasts.

S. Yes. But, before that, when you're going through the window, you are an erect penis. Does that sound right? Yet it doesn't do anything once it gets through the window. You know penises in a way I don't. For you a penis can go away, and still you don't get left with anything incomplete or complete. It's enough just to be an erection. I guess that's what you are: you are a phallus, which is different from a penis. A penis is something that really exists; a phallus is a symbol. And as you walk toward that house, you've got breasts and a belly and a vagina and a uterus out of which babies came. You—now listen to me because this is really grotesque, I mean you're grotesque when you do that: a woman, a complete biological woman in her underwear is walking toward a house saying that she's a prick, a penis, a phallus rather. It's grotesque. That is, if you really want to be *you*, then you've got to be embarrassed [p. 182] . . . for having shown me that you, who are a woman, were a phallus. As you walk up the driveway to that house, you deny your self. How can you do that to yourself? The answer is: you have to. But how can you deprive yourself even during those few minutes? You're not a phallus. Why do you want to cry?

G. I don't know. Just because I'm relieved or something. [Silence.]

Next hour.

S. The thing you steal is the most real thing in the world, isn't it? Nothing could be more solid and substantial. It's just the right size. It isn't a great thing . . . it's little. Is it something female? [Shakes head yes.] Is it a feminine object always, something that a woman has? [Shakes head no.]

G. I don't know. I was thinking of children's things. The music box, a doll in a glass case, a little . . . a picture of a mother and a child.

S. O.K. So the object has something to do with your relationship with your mother.

G. Oh, come on, leave my mother alone, will you? Leave me and my mother alone. I'm tired of my mother. I want nothing more to do with her. Why does it always have to be my mother? Why couldn't it be my aunt or my grandmother or . . . You know my mother steals things too. [This has never come out before.] I guess everybody does that. No, I guess everybody doesn't do it. She never goes to a restaurant or to a motel or any place without taking something . . . ash trays or something. Her house is full of shit that she's stolen. We all steal. The whole family steals. My father used to steal . . . funny things, you know. One time he stole a truck of oranges—I'll never forget that. I don't know . . . [Chuckles] . . .

S. What have you stolen from your mother?

G. Nothing. Money. I stole money from her. Lots of times. (I'm going to go. I am. I don't want to hear this bullshit. Let me put my boots on . . . and get out of here.) I never stole anything from my mother except money, and since that was the only thing she valued, that was very pertinent. (I've got a cramp in my toe again and it's your fault.) I stole money. She would hide it. She would go through all these horrible rituals to keep me away from her money, and I always got it. She knew it was me. I can remember I was six or seven years old—this was the first time—and she sent me to the store to get bread and I lost the money. So she said, "You stole it." And I said, "I didn't," and she said, "You did, and if you don't tell me, I'm going to beat you"; so I said, "I did."

S. And so you won.

G. Right.

S. And after that you tried to steal from her.

G. Right.

S. Because if she said you were going to steal, you might as well steal and get the fun of it.

G. My mother was always right. I stole it and stole it. And money was so precious to her: "Oh, my God!" A dime—you'd think her life depended on that dime —maybe it did, I don't know. She had five kids she was trying to feed.

S. And what you stole [when entering homes] was nickels and dimes kind of stuff—isn't that true?

G. Yeah. Do you know what I used to do with the money?

S. It always has to be in your hand [I guess]. What did you do with that money when I handed it to you the other day?

G. I held it until I spent it.

S. But you didn't . . . I didn't even know how to describe it when it happened—you didn't take it like a bill and put it in a pocket or fold it up or anything else; you took it and you crumpled it up instantly so that it became a part of your fist.

G. When I gave it to the lady at the store, it was wet.

S. Yeah. So now I understand. When you go into a house and pick something up, you hold it in your hand and you don't let go of it until—when? . . . After the ice cream? You can't go into the ice-cream place and eat ice cream and hold it . . . the object in your hand.

G. Do you want to bet?

S. Is that right? No, you don't hold it. You put it down and you look at it while you're eating.

G. I hold it in my hand.

S. Throughout the whole ice cream?

G. Right, like this [big fist].

S. We're getting more of the ritual; *none* of it is casual.

G. Right.

S. So then you get up and you pay for your ice cream and you go out and you get fucked. What happens to the object?

G. I put it down.

S. When you're getting fucked, you can't hold on to it.

G. I could.

S. At which point do you put it down?

G. After I go to get fucked. When I'm in the car, I put it down. I put it on the back seat; I don't want to look at it. I don't want any part of it.

S. When you're in the bar, let's say with the man [picking up the phallic stranger], you're sitting there with a drink in one hand and the object in the other. What have you done with it?

G. When I go to the bar . . .

S. Oh, I see. When the man part of it starts [on the way to finding a man], then you throw it on the back seat. Is that the end of it? That quickly? The same night it's already done except in rare instances you've kept them a little longer. The rare instances must have been something really mother-and-childish. How long did you keep the drawing [of mother and child]?

G. Quite awhile.

S. How long?

G. Three weeks.

S. What's the longest you've ever kept anything?

G. Three weeks.

S. What's the next longest?

G. I don't know.

S. The music box?

G. A couple of weeks. Why don't you join the police department?

S. It's similar. Tell me more about stealing money from your mother.

G. I'm wondering what the hell you're talking about. I would take the money and go out and spend it—not on me, on my friends. I didn't give a shit about the money. Money didn't mean anything to me. She was just out of her mind trying to figure out places to put that money where I couldn't get it [laughs].

S. Isn't that sort of the feeling you have when you're in the houses . . . that you'll find what you want no matter where they put it?

G. Right. It used to be a whole ritual about her hiding the money and me finding it. And I didn't always take it all. I didn't take it all. If there were fifteen dollars there, I took ten dollars.

S. To indicate that she had been ripped off.

G. Oh, it was a good indication because I took three-quarters of it. I stole it to rip off my mother and get her right where she lived and she lived in that fifteen dollars or whatever it was. "What are we going to do? I'm so tired and I work so hard. What are we going to do with no money?" She was talking to everybody in general. She never discussed it with me.

S. I think you'll be relieved if you can remember that the most terrible thing there is for you is your mother ripping you off, cheating you—as a baby . . . and ever since.

G. I don't know; I don't know about her cheating me as a baby. I know some of it. I know that my mother rips me off every opportunity she gets. She does it so quietly. Just a word or a look. I think it's something a little different, though like that. And what it is is that I have to steal when somebody makes me feel like I'm not a woman. Prior to my stealing, somebody will make some remark or some comment or look at me or do something to indicate they might be confused about whether . . . at least it confuses me: am I masculine or feminine, am I a male or a female? Calling somebody on a phone and them mistaking me for a man. Some remarks that my mother might make. But if somebody did that every day, I wouldn't have to steal every day. It seems like it builds.

The impulse to steal disappeared at this point and is still not there, several years later. Although the sense of being deprived recurs, she finally is conscious of what the deprivation is, and with the ritual of stealing exposed for her own inspection, she can look for more direct— and less dangerous and hostile—gratifications. These days, she turns to people and draws from them emotions of love her mother could not give her in the past. And other things are in place, too: Mrs. G. knows now that she is a person, not a penis, and that one need not perform one's sexual acts in the tight-fitting windows of suburban homes but with the living bodies of lovers. How unfortunate for people when the obvious must be disguised and the bearable truth registered as unbearable.

Because I have shown elsewhere (146) how Mrs. G. created her penis, masculinity, and homosexuality, perhaps a few words will suffice here. As seems true with other women who have strong yearnings to be male—the mothers of male transsexuals (chap. 8) and female transsexuals (147)—a dreadful disruption occurs in childhood that separates the girl from her mother, who becomes unreachable. Their mothers teach the girls— Mrs. G. and these others—that femaleness is worthless, and then, as for instance when brothers are favored, unbearable envy of males is created. These girls become adults: the mothers of transsexuals satisfy this penis envy when they grow their own beautiful phallus, the transsexual-to-be; the female transsexuals do so by the hormonal and surgical "sex change," which includes a phallus being literally sewn to their bodies. Mrs. G. both grew a penis (via hallucination) and made her whole body into one.

It was her good fortune to lose her need to have and to be a penis; in doing so, she also lost the craving that manifested itself in stealing.

Part III

Social Issues

Chapter 10

Is Homosexuality a Diagnosis?

Since homosexuality is the subject on which many social issues are fought, could it not be the central feature for a study of perversion, a word whose very connotations reek of moral, that is, social, issues? Of course. But because of its complexity and murkiness as an object of study (and especially because there are many conditions in which homosexual behavior occurs), I have kept homosexuality to the side in this search for the meaning of perversion. That cannot be done, however, in regard to social issues, since homosexuality is so pertinent at present. And because it is important, I am troubled at the way this vexatious issue is argued; it is too important to be decided by cleverness, faulty data, authoritarianism, or sophistry. Short-term gains won by noise, wit, or cunning in time diminish the worthiest causes.

I doubt that anyone yet is expert enough to tell us what to do about the social issues raised by psychiatric diagnoses, because no one can know what would happen as the years passed even if suggestions for social engineering were to be acted upon. While we can affect social issues by such jerry-building as is done with psychiatric diagnoses, in time the price paid is too high—and unnecessary. The same attitude applies to all the sexual aberrations—variants and perversions—in which the perverse person does not physically harm his partner or does not, as in the seduction of children, the mentally defective, or the psychotic, take his pleasure by force or other undue influence.

A diagnosis is a word or phrase that labels a condition. "Diagnosis" also has a second meaning: the process of collecting and abstracting data to arrive at a diagnosis. Because the validity of many psychiatric diagnoses (as distinct from other medical diagnoses) has been questioned over the years, we should try to evaluate our whole system of classifying. This, however, is a loaded subject. Homosexuals, victims of the use of diagnosis for oppression—from insult to denial of civil rights—will not be concerned with the esoterica of criteria for diagnosis; instead most of them will wish the term "homosexual" removed, not because it fails as a diagnosis, but because it can be used malevolently. (Since even using the term might suggest a diagnostic impulse, I note that "homosexual" is used herein only to imply that the person prefers sexual relations with someone of the same sex.)

But we really should separate out in our thinking these two trains of thought—diagnostic precision and diagnoses as social forces—or we shall suffer the kind of rambunctious discussion that makes a good show but overrides more serious purposes; for while both lines of argument are worthy, each is a different subject requiring different data and logic. If the two get mixed together, we shall blunder about as we usually do when social issues—matters of passion and action—are disguised as scientific or procedural issues. Being trained to think about phenomenology and the process of making diagnoses but not trained to unravel social issues, I shall concentrate especially on the former, leaving to those more knowledgeable the exciting revelations of Social Truth.

Criteria for Diagnosing

Were we not driven to it, we would no more choose homosexuality than any other alleged diagnosis as the subject upon which to fight the battle about the validity of psychiatric diagnoses. On resolving the general issues, we could then easily judge the claim to existence of most items within each category of the nomenclature: psychoses, neuroses, character disorders, or the jumble of loose pieces, including sexual disorders, that these three cannot contain. Most are just labels.

For instance, the neuroses, the sexual deviations, alcoholism, or drug dependence. In a painfully simpleminded fashion each of these is named for a distinctive feature; to tag someone, we come down hard on whatever catches the eye most, unable to deal with much of the rest that occurs inside the patient. Of course such a system is doomed to an unhappy life; tinkering every decade or so has not helped. It is comparable to a classification designed for the rest of medicine that would feature such "diagnoses" as cough, fever, headache, chronic indigestion, general weakness, vapors, or dyspepsia. No more and no less should most psychiatric "diagnoses" also be dropped. But if they are dropped, there is no more nomenclature. With no nomenclature, we have no place to start communicating about treatment or research.

Let me review what I think a diagnosis is, and in doing so show not only why no system of classification at present works in psychiatry but also why one does pretty well for the rest of medicine. A diagnosis is supposed to be a highly compact explanation. To make a proper diagnosis in any branch of medicine there should be: (1) a syndrome—a constellation of signs and symptoms shared by a group of people, visible to an observer; (2) underlying dynamics (pathogenesis)—pathophysiology in the rest of medicine, neuropathophysiology or psychodynamics in psychiatry; (3) etiology—those factors from which the dynamics originate. When these exist, we can save time by using shorthand, knowing that a word or two—a label, a diagnosis—communicates to others what we know. Unfortunately for psychiatrists, we are usually not confronted with people whose thinking, feelings, and behavior can be so categorized. Except for the disorders that are "diseases" in much the same sense as the term is used in the rest of medicine—such as the organic brain syndromes, which may include some of the schizophrenias and affective psychoses—the conditions for which our specialty was developed do not usually fulfill these three criteria. And so, should foregoing be a proper way to look at the structure of diagnosis (others think so [49]), the present system of classification is deeply flawed.

We might even debate whether the diagnostic system should be junked entirely, as a few have suggested. The price might be too great, but I must admit a flickering temptation to see that happen; it seems logical that if the shorthand that is a diagnosis is not a shared communication among those who use it, then it can only serve to confuse and might be better replaced for a time by descriptions. We shall not wipe out the classification system, however, and so psychiatry will persist, going down the list of the diagnoses one by one, year after year, testing the popularity of the items—the priorities determined as much by social as by scientific issues. Our problems with the nomenclature measure how far we must still travel for psychiatry to be grounded in scientific methodology. But it is too bad we go about the task piecemeal; to isolate homosexuality from the rest of the tottering system—unless everyone understands that the particular example is to serve only to illuminate the general issues—is to ignore the palsy from which the whole, necessarily inept, structure suffers.

So, we should not single out "homosexuality" because that diagnosis brings anguish to those diagnosed. The latter effect indicates important social issues, but our argument will be confused if we claim to talk of diagnosis and in fact turn out to be talking about the way diagnoses can be used corruptly. Many homosexuals today feel that the very diagnosis "homosexuality" serves, in the hands of psychiatrists (who should know better) and the public (which does not care to know better), as a hammer to oppress people whose only crime is their sexual style. I agree: to the extent that society does this and psychiatrists allow themselves to serve in this way, an injustice is committed that injures homosexuals and degrades psychiatrists. But a diagnosis should not be invalidated for that reason.

If one uses the three criteria above for considering a condition a diagnosis, homosexuality is not a diagnosis: (1) there is only a sexual preference (so noticeable because it frightens many in our society), not a uniform constellation of signs and symptoms; (2) different people with this sexual preference have different psychodynamics underlying their sexual behavior; and (3) quite different life experiences can cause these dynamics and this behavior. There *is* homosexual behavior; it is varied. People with all sorts of personality types prefer homosexuality as their sexual practice: people without overt neurotic symptomatology, schizophrenics, obsessive-compulsives, alcoholics, people with other perversions— almost every category in the nomenclature. But there is no such *thing* as homosexuality. In that sense it should be removed from the nomenclature.

As regards pathogenesis, probably no one these days —not even among those favoring the diagnosis—believes in a unitary cause for homosexual behavior; that would make it a *thing.* The fine reviews of the literature on etiology by Bieber et al. and Socarides, plus their own findings (3, 130), reinforce the impression that many paths lead to one's preferring members of one's own sex. This is true even, and especially, with analytic theories of etiology.

Should a diagnosis be dropped because it causes pain?

There is something disreputable in using our feeble method of diagnosis and psychiatrists en masse as the whipping boys for the cruel manner in which homosexuals have been and still are treated. These are not the real source of the mistreatment of homosexuals, (though they can be borrowed for such use). At our best, we, since Freud's lead, are partly responsible for the fact that homosexuals can begin fighting back against society. Even when we are inaccurate in calling homosexuality a diagnosis, doing so has signified that the homosexual is part of the natural realm and not a member of the species of damned sinners.

The oppressed, as they find their strength, may see there are two truths—usually unrelated—that their cause embodies. The first is the morality of their oppressed state and the factual falsifications told by one side (or the other) in order to remove (or maintain) an oppression; the first truth will be that the oppression is evil (or good). The oppressed are always the victims of definitions.

The second truth—the search for reality (scientific method)—we can put aside for the moment while we touch on the first—one's conviction that one's cause is righteous. The homosexual's stance is made more honorable, or at least more poignant, by the public's cruelty. In fact, there would be no diagnosis of homosexuality— only the myriad forms of homosexual behavior would be recognized—if the bigotry of the righteous did not force the belief (shared even by homosexuals) that a distinct essence—homosexuality—exists.

Some of society's hatred for sexuality is unwarranted because unprovoked, such as its concern over which orifices of which sex are used. This hatred is mostly our cultural heritage. But another part, having little to do with the homosexual act of intercourse, the homosexual (usually male) provokes by conscious design; he contributes—he even enjoys contributing—to his own oppression. For multiple, complicated reasons, many homosexuals are committed to clowning, mimicry, caricature, whenever an audience—heterosexual or homosexual—is present. An ingredient of these performances is sarcasm—hostility—in which there is a joke: "When I seem to be making fun of myself, I am actually making fun of the straight world—with the additional bonus that they are too dumb even to know what I am doing to them."

Although it is true the public does not know quite what is being done to it, it cannot help but sense that it is being toyed with; so it gets angry and charges its tormentor like a bull. That attack may damage the homosexual, but even as he is hurt, he also feels superior, because *he* is not a bull—a blind, stupid animal. Rather, he is an aesthete—a tweaker, not a charger.

Many homosexuals learned these and other methods of coping from the skirmishes lost in childhood to their parents. Some homosexuals are defeated mostly by their blackmailing mothers, with their fathers simply supplying a passive idiocy; that could hardly encourage a son to emulate such a father. Others, brutalized by rage-blurred fathers, run away and hide themselves inside the guise of their wretched mothers' mannerisms. (These two examples are not meant to explain the origins of homosexual behavior, although I do think factors like these, plus many more, can contribute.) In any case, there is plenty of cause for revenge, which, I believe, energizes aspects of many homosexuals' behavior, erotic and otherwise. And thus, in order to salvage a sense of value from foci of despair, they must strike back at all who have qualities like the old enemies of their childhood. These mechanisms, though in different forms and degrees, may be found in nonhomosexuals as well; masochism is not the domain only of homosexuals. Once again, I do not offer these ideas as full explanations.

Three mechanisms used by homosexuals that provoke volleys of hatred fired at them by the straights are:

1. Homosexuals transfer hatred directed originally at
parents onto parent surrogates in society—and the surrogates strike back.

2. Homosexuals, taught self-hatred in childhood, persist in attracting punishment because in part they agree
with the cruel straight society; they provoke attack in
order to be humiliated.

3. Homosexuals can threaten the heterosexual stance
of the militant straight, bullying him with insight into his
own homosexual or effeminate potentials. To prove himself, the heterosexual may retaliate.

These dynamics of hostility are, I believe, characteris-
tic of male more than of female homosexuality. For instance, one does not see much mimicry in the masculine
behavior of females,* but it is an essential part of the
effeminacy of males. It is generally believed that female
homosexuality has for millennia been ignored by cultures because women were beneath each society's con-
tempt—and concern. That may not be all; women
homosexuals, less openly raucous and hostile toward
their oppressors than most homosexual men, draw down
on themselves little attack. Or at least that was the case
until recently.

To return from our detour: the first truth, then, is the
immorality of oppression. The second truth, less important in the crises of the oppressed, is, I believe, nonetheless also a social cause that, over the long haul, has its
own rightful importance. It is the scientific method, a
beautifully constructed set of rules—and a dependable
conscience for each researcher and his own corruptible
conscience—that guides the effort to find facts. It
(though not necessarily a particular scientist) represents
a larger truth: that honesty has long-term social value for
mankind and must be protected, encouraged, and taught
and its methodology forever refined. The process of

*Is this related to the female's knowing she is a female like her
mother?

diagnosis in medicine—a process of detection—is a piece of this scientific method. And so we look for etiology.

In the search for the multiple causes of homosexual behavior, data can be found demonstrating that, for many homosexuals, their preferences in object choice and some of their essential, habitual nonerotic behavior (such as the effeminacy of male homosexuals) were developed as the result of trauma and frustration during childhood. These observations also hold for most heterosexuals, though the traumas and frustrations are of different sorts and intensities.

If one divides humans into two types, heterosexuals and others, as is the custom, we can sort the two in the following idiosyncratic manner (rather as Freud did): the sexual habits of most humans, including most who prefer homosexual relations, are heterosexual. (Heterosexuality may of course also contain homosexuality.) The erotic neuroses—the obvious perversions and even most variations of overt heterosexuality, such as compulsive promiscuity, use of pornography, preference for prostitutes, and adult masturbation—are heterosexual distortions, compromises, filled nonetheless with excitement, that allow one to give up certain desires if only others can be salvaged. If it makes the oppressed minorities more comfortable, we can all be given a diagnosis; such a pronouncement would certainly not often distort the case. Everyone has his own style or distinctive fantasy that he daydreams or stages with objects; everyone is entitled to a category.

But why claim that heterosexuality is mankind's preference? Many maintain that heterosexuality is the biologically natural state in man: first, because it is so in all other species, and second, because only it can prevent the species from dying out. Yet there is no direct evidence for this biological propensity in man other than the seemingly overwhelming fact that most people are, more or less, heterosexual. While there is no reason to deny there may be some such biological tendency, we know that psychological events can so often overthrow this latent heterosexuality that considering it biologically fixed is a weak foundation on which to build a theory or a society. Perhaps an even stronger force pressing toward heterosexuality in humans is the make-up of the family, which may have been invented, not because of biological heterosexuality, but for life-and-death realities that have plagued existence to the present. As personal safety and comfort increase, some sense that the next casualty after God may be the family.

In saying that the family is more effective in promoting heterosexuality than any biological urge, I mean the following. Every child knows that he is the product of an inevitably heterosexual act that is intimate, exciting, mysterious, astonishing, profound, dangerous, forbidden, and terribly desirable; and every family—even those whose failure produces severe disorder in the child immersed in it—unendingly blankets its offspring with messages that the ideal would be a heterosexual family. However restrictive the myth of heterosexuality may be, however much sex militants hate it, and however bitter people are at how far its reality has fallen below perfection, heterosexuality with love—affection, respect, honesty, decreased selfishness, long-lasting erotic interest and lustful gratification, fidelity, joy in children, and creation of a unit larger and more original than the two people making it up—is the criterion. This is so not because it is ordained so by heaven, biology, or economic theory but because almost all members of our society accept it somewhere within themselves as the ideal that haunts them.

So perversions (but not all sexual aberrances) are modifications one must invent in order to preserve some of one's heterosexuality. The form the perversion takes may be far from the extreme of a male preferring a female and vice versa, with both wholeheartedly enjoying the sexual and loving aspects of their relationship.

Yet, while unseen, that ideal is buried there in most of us even if manifest in only a few.

Now, to return to the idea that diagnoses can be used to push people around. I would still suggest that any diagnosis—not just "homosexuality"—be removed from our classification only when we can prove the condition does not exist, not because the diagnosis may cause pain. That being the case, we have a responsibility to define precisely each of the alleged diagnoses in our classification, for with proper definition, we can determine whether what has been defined in fact exists. Perhaps in time this will occur in a number of conditions now called homosexuality, wherein one's preferred sexual object is of the same sex. We shall then have a number of subdiagnoses within a major category, "the homosexualities."

Someday we may know enough to be able to diagnose as does the rest of medicine. On the other hand, we may come to see diagnosis as an illusory occupation when dealing with human identity. In the meantime, I would suggest that we drop diagnosing used only to underline either the most flamboyant sexual behavior (which may have been only a momentary act) or even the preferred sexual behavior, just because the person does not habitually join genitals with someone of the opposite sex.

We can be so clever: we secrete our insults in our grammar. To say, "He is *a* neurotic" is more absolute than to say, "He is neurotic"; with the first, we have made him synonymous with his neurosis. If, either to be kind or to be accurate, we say, "He *has* a neurosis," we lessen our chances of being unpleasant. Now suppose that, wanting to communicate accurately and succinctly, we were to say, "He has a homosexuality": the power of the words to insult is weakened. We are no longer saying either that his sexual customs are the totality of his being or that we—the grand arbiters—simply have no interest in the rest of his personality. A touch of the golden rule might improve our diagnostic habits.

Could we try this: as a holding action, until the day

when we know what we are doing, if the circumstances require that a psychiatric label be given, we proceed in this way:

A. *The personality (character) type habitual since childhood, or adolescence,* for example, obsessive compulsive, schizophrenic, hysteric, depressive.

   1. *The presenting syndrome,* for example, drug dependence, anxiety neurosis, schizophreniform psychosis.

      a. *Subsidiary syndromes also present,* for example, alcoholism, nonpsychotic OBS with senile brain disease; psychophysiologic respiratory disorder (asthma).

         (1) *Sexual preference,* for example, heterosexual, monogamous, with accompanying fantasies of being raped by a stallion; homosexual, with foreskin fetishism; heterosexual, with preference for cadavers; homosexual, with disembodied penises (tearoom promiscuity); heterosexual, voyeurism; homosexual, expressed only in fantasies during intercourse with wife.

The advantage of this syndrome classificatory system is that it does not pretend to be a diagnostic system, that is, explanatory. It admits its ignorance: it is descriptive.

This position holds for both disputants, the oppressed and the oppressors (including of course some psychiatrists): diagnoses should not be thrown out because someone is upset by being labeled, and they should not be retained because they can be used to oppress. Neither extreme honors the function of diagnosis. Only when diagnoses fail to describe succinctly and accurately should they be removed. Since that is the case with homosexuality, it cannot yet function as a true diagnosis: we should remove it. And since that is true for most of the rest of the "diagnoses" of psychiatry, let us scrap the system (though not yet all the labels) and start afresh.

Chapter 11

Sex as Sin

Let us start with an ancient thesis: everyone experiences the sexual act as a question of morality. Having examined how hostility, mystery, risk, and revenge can increase excitement, we can see why.

For our present purpose, in which we are concerned only with erotism, let me define sin as the exalted term for the desire to harm others. Ethics and morality, then, are scales society uses for weighing sin, and they exist to justify or mitigate hostility. In demonstrating that hostility plays an essential role in forming and maintaining human sexual excitement, I was also, subliminally, studying some of the dynamics of ethics and morality.

Placing hostility in the center of these definitions puts me somewhat at odds with those who explain sin in sexual pleasure only as a cultural-historical phenomenon. The latter construction describes this sense of sin as the product of a Judeo-Christian heritage, fortified in each different generation and place by local conditions in the service of bigots. If one uses this explanation, the solution for the suffering caused by such repressive forces is simple to conceive (though difficult to effect): when one changes the beliefs of society, the sense of sin will dissipate.

Perhaps. But while we await that happy day, remembering that inner life is not only a result but a cause of culture, let us also look at the dynamics of sexual pleasure *within* a person. On doing so, we may find that some of the repressive social forces—experienced inside the individual as a sense of sin—have their origin in attacks made by one part of oneself upon another part (such as the bite of conscience); social forces do not just exist outdoors in the wind but, in the final common pathway for each member of society, are present as intrapsychic dynamics.

It is hard in enlightened circles these days to defend the idea that sex and sin are linked. Is there, then, no logical basis for the badness, strangeness, willfully motivated corruptness, unwholesomeness, and unnaturalness that, sadly, people feel in their sexual excitement?

In answering, we may find our first clue in the long-known fact that an awareness that one is sinning often increases sexual excitement. For more evidence, we can look to the thesis suggested by the data in this book that when certain permutations of hostility and dehumanization of one's desired object are not mixed in, for most people a dull lump of meager pleasure replaces enthusiastic lust. Feeling sinful does not come mainly from effects as superficial as the culturalist explanation has it —that is, it is not just an imposition cruelly laid on one by mindless society—but rather comes also from one's being at least faintly aware that some of sexual excitement depends on the desire to harm others. Studying perversion shows this mechanism at work and has led me to more understanding of the lesser aberrations, which are usually referred to as "normal sexuality."

In both perversion and "normal sexuality" we have found several themes: as the sexual act unfolds, fantasy risks are run that are experienced as being surmounted; inside the sexual excitement are desires—conscious and unconscious—to harm others in order to get revenge for past traumas and frustrations; the sexual act serves to transform childhood trauma into adult triumph; trauma, risk, and revenge establish a mood of excitement that is intensified when they are packaged as mystery.

The ideas just reviewed serve only to complement our knowledge of the origins of sin in the conflicts arising out of the earliest stages of infantile and childhood development, arranged conceptually as oral, anal, phallic, and oedipal. The ruthless possessiveness and destructive urges of early life, more or less encapsulated by those psychic experiences we call the superego, provide data and a framework essential for understanding the sense of sin. Attending to the anger and cruelty that arise in the early frustrations and traumas allows us to trace how these feelings and their accompanying sense of victimization are converted to sexual pleasure.

This knowledge of the dynamics of hostility in excitement can lead those so inclined into concerns about ethics and morality, since these latter institutions deal with the modulation of hostility among individuals or inside the mind of each. If ethics and morality serve society by defining and dealing with sin, then this exploration of sexual excitement suggests that the ethics and morality of sexual behavior intuitively probe to reach and subdue these dynamics of hostility. Perhaps if this probing can be raised to consciousness, we can decrease the hostility—which in the extreme reaches levels of perversion—that the ethical and moral systems of reform use as a counterforce to sin. And as a strategy of social action perhaps those who wish to increase sexual freedom ought not to lean too heavily on the argument that the sense of sin exists only as an effect of one's enslavement by repressive historical processes. The sense of sin may not disappear simply because we announce that it is outdated, and the complex richness of human sexual excitement will be missed if we exclude sin from our studies.

If these ideas on perversion were accepted, the function of the courts would be simpler. If it was known that almost all sexual behavior has in it traces of the perversion mechanism and therefore that perverse impulses and acts are universal (this is, of course, already known, though not yet acknowledged in the law), the criterion for decision about crime need not be: Was perversion present? Instead—a more sensible, just way to define a crime—a judge or jury need only decide if a hostile act had been committed that caused damage to persons or property in the degree that the penal code feels is significant for nonsexual crimes; let the same criterion hold.

This would be a decision not requiring "expert"—psychiatric—opinions.

Of course, this discussion falls into absurdity if we forget that all sins are not equal. The fantasy of rape is not rape, and the transvestite's unconscious fantasy of revenge leads to nothing more violent than his masturbating into a lady's hat. The presence of the sense of sin, therefore, may not be related to real violence, and fortunately the laws governing sexual behavior, though usually dim-witted, sometimes take this into account.

Psychoanalysts take to discussing morals and ethics like drunkards to drink. I do not wish to serve as one more grand master of sexual behavior, to judge if sexual freedom damages or enriches society, or to pronounce what laws should be created and how enforced to reflect our morality. But there is one concern I think is worthy of emphasis: if we deny the hostility and dehumanization in the fantasies that make for sexual excitement—if we say sin is not there—we are denying the obvious, and that is foolish.

There are those for whom, in their orthodoxy, sin and personal responsibility are the keystone of the structure of society: each of us shall know, weigh, and harvest the consequences of our behavior. The thesis, then, that sexual excitement and the need to harm one's objects are closely related makes control of sex not only the domain of personal dynamics but at the same time a political affair.

Those nonfanatics who think in terms of sex as sin start from a position similar to mine: when, out of anxiety, we dehumanize our sexual objects, we minimize ourselves and forgo the best of being human—the capacity to love. Thus, believe the ones who hold this most vehemently, it hardly serves society to encourage its own dissolution by propaganda for libertinism, by pornography, by loosening the laws, or by laboratory research on human sexual behavior (67). On the other hand, if we discourage dehumanization by curbing unlimited infantile sexuality in children, adolescents, and adults, our reward will be the power of love. Such a stand is courageous if not almost suicidal, for, in opposing the right to perversion, they try to impede a powerful impulse now moving our society. Those who articulate such conservatism not only ask for attack from the new intellectual and moral majorities on the left, but they must also abide, as colleagues, the political cannonballs on the right who for generations have held the same ground they defend.

Theoretical support for such argument comes from two groups that usually do not lie down together: the inspirational psychologists (such as May, Polanyi, and Frankl) and the psychoanalysts (such as Freud and Khan). From the first persuasion, whose basic premise is that man is good when not corrupted, is drawn the moral strength to ask for "sanctions" to preserve this good, with the argument that love, with its lasting commitment to another's presence, requires sexual restraint. And so, if we are to preserve what is most valuable in human relations, we must oppose the enemy of love—sexual license ("fascistic," "schizoid," "delusional" [67]).

The second ideology, psychoanalysis, demonstrates that hostility lies at the center of perversion and thus can serve to strengthen the conviction of those who feel that the present increase of sexual freedom is evil (see [76] for a review). Freud's discovery that sexual aberrations result from traumatic disruption of infantile development serves as the background. Khan's findings have broadened our understanding of the meaning and function of perversions, such as the use of others as things (dehumanization) rather than as people and as objects of envy and greed instead of love; the use of manipulative techniques of intimacy to exploit partners in perversion; the falsification of one's self; and perversion as an act rather than a true relationship between people (75, 76). One cannot doubt, after a review of such findings, that perversion is not—in the way a variant is—just "an alternative way of life," as some apologists today would have it. The argument is clearly made, as it has been since Freud, that capacity for sexual pleasure in perversion can be retained only with some sacrifice of the humanness of one's objects and by crippling one's self. When one must reduce people to things, love—with its binding of hatred —cannot persist.

These, then, are the two pieces used to construct the conservative thesis: first, that unchecked sexuality dehumanizes erotic life and thus thwarts love, and second, that the need to dehumanize, which has its origins in traumatic, conflict-laden childhood experiences, is built from hostility.

I agree, yet disapprove of the solution to which the conservatives come: punish. They are law-and-order men. Their call for action requires, in the absence of a population of mature people capable of nonperverse loving, acts of repression by society upon its citizens to force containment of perversity. But maturity—despite what political philosophers hope—is hardly ever the product of political action, and the psychoanalyst cannot help but imagine the forms perversion and its attendant hatred take when driven underground. If only love could be created in a populus by sexual restraint; but when has there been a civilization whose health was the result of suppression of unlimited sexuality? (When was there— what is—a healthy civilization?) If only love did not also require the dynamics of infancy and childhood; if only it could be created *de novo* in adults by exhortation and law. If only it were true that love is so inherent in people that we could count on its emergence with a few tightenings of the law. If only neurosis were an aberration and less part of the state of man. This demand for restraint is no more than modestly utopian; it is not hard to believe that the less hatred there is in intimacy the happier the outcome for the participants. But the program for turning hatred to love by police action has not been a successful experiment in the past. Besides—as others have noted— utopias are calm but dull (and dangerous); without the perverse—those who cannot bear sustained intimacy —we may be denied most of our artists, scientific discoverers, moral leaders, political geniuses, and great philosophers.

While I agree that there is less perversion in a relationship where there is more love, that is my private belief; I could not prove it, and no one else has. Yet, if one is to state such beliefs publicly, one has to be convincing. The issues are too important. Before we reduce freedom of speech or the rights of consenting adults to privacy, including privacy to engage in aberrant sexual behavior, the argument must be a match for the risks we are asked to run. Here is what I need in order to be convinced: some demonstration that the mass of mankind is inherently good and that its capacity for love rather than hatred can be harnessed *now*, not in some unstated future; a worthy description of what is meant by love between two people, so that I can judge whether it is worth more to our society—right now, in these dangerous times— than the freedom of press and speech and the right to private perversion we are asked to limit; a reasonable demonstration that this love is available—now, by some route that can be revealed—to most people, so that this means of saving society can be instituted; some demonstration that if perversion and hostility will not go away, punitive laws will either dissipate these conditions or drive them underground without their still being dangerous; guidelines on how we should call up the forces of repression and then soften them before these forces, and especially the people who will take the power of repression into their own hands, go further than the sorcerer's apprentices would want. I am uneasy with the idea that the prime solution to the problem of corruption is that man's inherent capacity to love will see us through but that till we can tap that love, we should take away some of his freedom.

I happen to agree (though not intensely) that pornography is debasing, that people would be better off nonperverse, that gorging on pregenital pleasures will make people frantic (or is it that frantic people are the ones who gorge?). I might even agree that licentiousness damages the fabric of society (though, in fact, I rather believe that licentiousness is more the result of a change in the fabric than the other way round). But, perhaps because I live in the United States of today, I am even more worried about repression of freedom than about the price we pay if we permit corruption. Our civilization has been traumatized in this century by the police state, and the United States is at this moment still so threatened by those who would tighten the laws that I would rather let freedom run a bit more before we panic.

There are, among others, two types of freedom. One is (relative) freedom from one's neurotic unconscious demands; that is lost in perversion. The other is the (relative) freedom a society can grant all its citizens. Both are precious, but in this time of emergency, I would try to save the latter first.

Chapter *12*

The Necessity
of Perversion

Until the family no longer functions as the primal unit in
the maintenance of society, perversion will serve four
necessities: preservation of the individual's pleasure,
preservation of the family, preservation of society, and
preservation of the species. In claiming this, I am moving
beyond Freud's fundamental discovery that the perverse
person is a *casualty* of that necessity of society, the family,
to the position that perversion is a *necessity* created by
society and the family so as not themselves to become
worse casualties.

The first necessity, preservation of pleasure, has been
discussed enough in this book; and it has been at the
heart of the theory and data of psychoanalysis since its
beginnings. So I can allow our common knowledge of
this factor—in case this book did not do its work well
enough—to speak for itself.

As we know from studying oedipal conflict, intimacy
causes erotic strains so severe that the family's stability
is chronically endangered. Thus a second necessity: perversion must act as a repository of conservatism to stabi-
lize otherwise explosive forces. It allows cruelty and
hatred in the family to be contained before they become

too destructive, and the resulting efficiency permits parents to secure themselves and their family by means of the presence of their perverse child. For instance, a future homosexual man's mother, in innumerable small doses, may release on her little boy her bitterness toward males in general and her unsatisfying husband in particular; in being distant and accepting her scorn without argument, her husband may be allowed to retain his passivity; and by developing a mimicking effeminacy, the boy can secretly despise his mother.

Additionally, scapegoating helps many families, who choose one member to serve as the "sick" or "evil" one, allowing projection to protect the other members as individuals as well as the whole family as a unit. Once this is done, parents can live out some of their perverse wishes in the chosen child (cf. 70). Then, too, perversion allows parents to play their assigned parts in the oedipal production, to preserve their own sexual pleasure, and to reinforce themselves in their uneasy role of parent. For this, their child's perversion is a sacrifice they are willing to make. In brief, perversion not only may be the price in neurosis paid for the institution that is the family, but also, when we turn the coin over, we find as its other side that perversion has served—as a counterrevolutionary force—to allow the family to persist.

Third, by preserving the family, perversion saves society, in all the forms the latter has taken so far in evolving over the millennia. And with the terrible strains laid upon society, especially in the last century, by the material successes of the Industrial Revolution, one can expect to see a reflex demand that perversion widen its counterrevolutionary function to save the present forms of society from the dissolution threatened by physical well-being. But it now looks as if the production of goods may soon reach the point that it will make obsolete for some countries certain formerly necessary functions of the family; more and more, progress provides protections to many who, in the past, could persist by means only the family could consistently provide: food, shelter, protection of the children, a bit of luxury, a few quiet moments. Equally important, birth control greatly reduces the frightful work load that massive procreation demanded. These changes may free the forces of perversion for more lighthearted services, such as the arts. And then, as usually happens with major social phenomena, something—like perversion or the methodology of science—that starts out as a defender of the status quo will gradually be elaborated, with scarcely a wrench, into a radical agent of change.

Perversion, thus, is to serve society's and the species' abiding changelessness. But a constant threat to *perversion's* smooth function is the *perverse person* and his paranoia. He who breaks the rules by refusing to play the part of pervert as written in society's mores and sanctions—who rebels against his assignment and will not help his neighbor by being clown and victim—may in time force social change, if not downright revolution.

A fourth necessity served by perversion is the survival of the species. Paradoxically, while its dynamics lead, in a few families, to the eventual destruction of children's capacity to reproduce, perversion, as Freud defined it and as we have discussed (chap. 10), is an effort at preserving heterosexuality.

While the oedipal situation, that product of the heterosexual family, damages emerging heterosexuality with its threats and anxieties, it also tantalizes the growing child with its possibilities for safety, affection, and physical pleasure. And so, I suggest along with others, neither heterosexuality nor the family is inevitable or eternal. Rather, both—primarily social creations—work to strengthen each other, and both have created their myths that each is an eternal verity (considered God-given by the religious and gene-given by the scientific).

In many cases, the desire for preserving the species is

retained only in the unconscious of the perverse—that victimized heterosexual *manqué;* but more frequently, the childhood trauma and frustration are resolved less drastically. A tattered heterosexuality remains so that the survivor of the family's dynamics can manage genitally, and in rare cases, can even succeed well enough to build in turn what society at present still demands: a family that will one day reproduce itself.

Additional advantages (though not necessities) accrue once perversion has been invented. For instance, since its central dynamic is hostility, perversion serves to channel murderous hatred out into the calmer currents of the imagination, such as religion, art, pornography, and daydreams. These deflections are almost always preferable to the direct expression of the forces they contain and trap in the unconscious. This dispersion of rage serves our four main necessities, by providing a more joyous and guilt-reduced erotic pleasure, by lowering the murder rate in families (both the family to which the child belonged and that formed by the child-become-adult), by binding into erotic pleasure and exhaustion energies that might otherwise break society open,* and by deflecting the hatred that can build up between the sexes so that, at least for a few moments, men and women can stand what too often seems each other's otherwise unbearable total presence.

In other words, like all other conditions produced by neurotic mechanisms so stabilized and efficient that we call them character structure, perversion serves as the only workable complex of compromises; it draws off enough rage and despair that society and the individual are not completely unstrung by the otherwise destructive tendencies arising from infantile frustration and trauma in the family.

*The preference of fanatical revolutionaries for sexual abstinence is a perversion that subdues the hostility present inside the family (party), letting it be released for destruction of those outside.

As long as there are infants, society will invent ways to raise them, and, in raising them, will shape their sexual desire. Not knowing what will come if the family disappears, we cannot know how human sexuality will, in adapting, be modified. My guess is that if all goes well for our race, perversion will die down and variance increase. Perhaps someday perversion will not be necessary.

References

1. BAK, R. C. "The Phallic Woman: The Ubiquitous Fantasy in Perversions." *Psychoanal. Study Child* 23 (1968): 15–36. New York: International Universities Press.
2. BANDURA, A., and WALTERS, R. H. *Social Learning and Personality Development*. New York: Holt, Rinehart & Winston, 1963.
3. BIEBER, I.; DAIN, H. J.; DINCE, P. R.; DRELLICH, M. G.; GRAND, H. G.; GUNDLACH, R. H.; KREMER, M. W.; RIFKIN, A. H.; WILBUR, C. B.; and BIEBER, T. B. *Homosexuality*. New York: Basic Books, 1962.
4. BILLER, A. B. "Father Absence and the Personality Development of the Male Child." *Developmental Psychology* 2 (1970): 181–270.
5. BLUMER, D. "Transsexualism, Sexual Dysfunction and Temporal Lobe Disorder." In *Transsexualism and Sex Reassignment*, ed. R. Green and J. Money, pp. 213–219. Baltimore: Johns Hopkins Press, 1969.
6. BOEHM, R. "The Femininity-Complex in Men." *Int. J. Psycho-Anal.* 11 (1930): 444–469.
7. BOSS, M. *Meaning and Content of Sexual Perversions*. New York: Grune & Stratton, 1949.
8. BOWLBY, J. *Attachment*. New York: Basic Books, 1969.
9. "Brain Surgery for Sexual Disorders." *Br. Med. J.* 2 (1969): 250.
10. BRODIE, H. K. H.; GARTRELL, N.; DOERING, C.; and RHUE, T. "Plasma Testosterone Levels in Heterosexual and Homosexual Men." *Am. J. Psychiat.* 131 (1974): 82–83.

11. CHODOFF, P. "A Critique of Freud's Theory of Infantile Sexuality." *Am. J. Psychiat.* 123 (1966): 507–518.

12. COOPER, A. J.; ISMAIL, A. A. A.; PHANJOO, A. L.; et al. "Antiandrogen (Cyproterone Acetate) Therapy in Deviant Hypersexuality." *Br. J. Psychiat.* 120 (1972): 59–63.

13. CRAMER, B. "Sex Differences in Early Childhood." *Child Psychiat. and Human Develop.* 1 (1971): 133–151.

14. DEVEREUX, G. "Panel Report: Perversion" (J. A. Arlow, reporter). *J. Am. Psychoanal. Assoc.* 2 (1954): 336–345.

15. DOERR, P.; KOCKOTT, G.; VOGT, H. J.; PIRKE, K. M.; and DITTMAR, F. "Plasma Testosterone, Estradiol, and Semen Analysis in Male Homosexuals." *Arch. Gen. Psychiat.* 29 (1973): 829–833.

16. EPSTEIN, A. W. "The Relationship of Altered Brain States to Sexual Psychopathology." In *Contemporary Sexual Behavior: Critical Issues in the 1970s,* ed. J. Zubin and J. Money, pp. 297–310. Baltimore: Johns Hopkins Press, 1973.

17. ESCALONA, S. K., and GORMAN, H. H. "Early Life Experience and the Development of Competence." *Int. Rev. Psychoanal.* 1 (1974): 151–168.

18. FENICHEL, O. (1930). "The Psychology of Transvestitism." In *Collected Papers.* New York: W. W. Norton & Co., 1953.

19. ———. *The Psychoanalytic Theory of Neurosis.* New York: W. W. Norton & Co., 1945.

20. FOX, C.; ISMAIL, A.; LOVE, D.; KIRKHAM, K.; and LORAINE, J. "Studies on the Relationship Between Plasma Testosterone Levels and Human Sexual Activity." *J. Endocrin.* 52 (1972): 51–58.

21. FREUD, A. *The Ego and the Mechanisms of Defense.* London: Hogarth Press, 1937.

22. ———. "The Infantile Neurosis: Genetic and Dynamic Considerations." *Psychoanal. Study Child* 26 (1971): 79–90. New York: International Universities Press.

23. FREUD, S. (1900). *The Interpretation of Dreams. Standard Edition* 4. London: Hogarth Press, 1953. *(Standard Edition* hereafter noted as *SE.)*

24. ——— (1905). *Three Essays on the Theory of Sexuality. SE* 7 (1953): 135–243.

25. ——— (1905). *Jokes and Their Relation to the Unconscious. SE* 8 (1960).

26. ——— (1909). "Analysis of a Phobia in a Five-Year-Old Boy." *SE* 10 (1955): 5–149.

27. ——— (1911). "Psycho-analytic Notes on an Autobiographical Account of a Case of Paranoia (Dementia Paranoides)." *SE* 12 (1958): 9–82.

28. ——— (1912). "The Dynamics of Transference." *SE* 12 (1958): 99–108.

29. ——— (1915). "Instincts and Their Vicissitudes." *SE* 14 (1957): 117–140.

30. ——— (1919). "A Child Is Being Beaten." *SE* 17 (1955): 179–204.

31. ——— (1923). *The Ego and the Id. SE* 19 (1961): 12–66.

32. ——— (1927). "Fetishism." *SE* 21 (1961): 152–157.

33. ——— (1932). "Femininity." *SE* 22 (1964): 112–135.

34. ——— (1937). "Analysis Terminable and Interminable." *SE* 23 (1964): 216–253.

35. ——— (1940). "The Splitting of the Ego in the Process of Defence." *SE* 23 (1964): 275–278.

36. FRIDAY, N. *My Secret Garden: Women's Sexual Fantasies.* New York: Trident Press, 1973.

37. GADPAILLE, W. J. "Research into the Physiology of Maleness and Femaleness." *Arch. Gen. Psychiat.* 26 (1972): 193–206.

38. GALENSON, E. "A Consideration of the Nature of Thought in Childhood Play." In *Separation-Individuation: Essays in Honor of Margaret S. Mahler,* ed. J. B. McDevitt and C. F. Settlage, pp. 41–59. New York: International Universities Press, 1971.

39. ———, and ROIPHE, H. "The Impact of Early Sexual Discovery on Mood, Defensive Organization, and Symbolization." *Psychoanal. Study Child* 26 (1972): 195–216. New York: Quadrangle Books, 1972.

40. GALLE, O. R.; GOVE, W. R.; and McPHERSON, J. M. "Population Density and Pathology: What Are the Relations for Man?" *Science* 176 (1972): 23–30.

41. GEBHARD, P. H.; GAGNON, J. H.; POMEROY, W. B.; et al.

Sex Offenders. New York: Harper & Row Publishers, 1965.

42. GILLESPIE, W. H. "A Contribution to the Study of Fetishism." *Int. J. Psycho-Anal.* 21 (1940): 401–415.

43. ———. "Notes on the Analysis of Sexual Perversions." *Int. J. Psycho-Anal.* 33 (1952): 397–402.

44. ———. "The General Theory of Sexual Perversion." *Int. J. Psycho-Anal.* 37 (1956): 396–403.

45. ———. "The Psycho-analytic Theory of Sexual Deviation with Special Reference to Fetishism." In *The Pathology and Treatment of Sexual Deviation: A Methodological Approach,* ed. I. Rosen, pp. 123–145. New York: Oxford University Press, 1964.

46. GLOVER, E. *The Roots of Crime.* New York: Hillary House Publishers, 1960.

47. ———. "Aggression and Sado-Masochism." In *The Pathology and Treatment of Sexual Deviation: A Methodological Approach,* ed. I. Rosen, pp. 146–162. New York: Oxford University Press, 1964.

48. GOLDBERG, S., and LEWIS, S. "Play Behavior in the Year-Old Infant: Early Sex Differences." *Child Devel.* 40 (1969): 21–33.

49. GOLDMAN, R. *Principles of Medical Science.* New York: McGraw-Hill Book Co., 1973.

50. GRAY, P. H. "Theory and Evidence of Imprinting in Human Infants." *J. Psychol.* 46 (1958): 155–166.

51. GREEN, R. "Homosexuality as a Mental Illness." *Int. J. Psychiat.* 10 (1972): 77–98.

52. ———. *Sexual Identity Conflict in Children and Adults.* New York: Basic Books, 1973.

53. GREENACRE, P. "Respiratory Incorporation and the Phallic Phase." *Psychoanal. Study Child* 6 (1951): 180–205. New York: International Universities Press.

54. ———. "Certain Relationships Between Fetishism and the Faulty Development of the Body Image." *Psychoanal. Study Child* 8 (1953): 79–98. New York: International Universities Press.

55. ———. "Further Considerations Regarding Fetishism." *Psychoanal. Study Child* 10 (1955): 187–194. New York: International Universities Press.

56. ———. "On Focal Symbiosis." In *Dynamic Psychopathology in Childhood,* ed. L. Jessner and E. Pavenstedt, pp. 243–256. New York: Grune & Stratton, 1959.

57. ———. "Further Notes on Fetishism." *Psychoanal. Study Child* 15 (1960): 191–207. New York: International Universities Press.

58. ———. "Perversions: General Considerations Regarding Their Genetic and Dynamic Background." *Psychoanal. Study Child* 23 (1968): 47–62. New York: International Universities Press.

59. ———. "The Fetish and the Transitional Object." *Psychoanal. Study Child* 24 (1969): 144–164. New York: International Universities Press.

60. GREENSON, R. R. "A Transvestite Boy and a Hypothesis." *Int. J. Psycho-Anal.* 47 (1966): 396–403.

61. ———. "Dis-identifying from Mother." *Int. J. Psycho-Anal.* 49 (1968): 370–374.

62. GREENSPAN, J., and MYERS, J. M., JR. "A Review of the Thoeretical Concepts of Paranoid Delusions with Special Reference to Women." *Penn. Psychiat. Quart.* 1 (1961): 11–28.

63. HARLOW, H. F., and HARLOW, M. K. "Social Deprivation in Monkeys." *Sci. Am.* 207 (1962): 136–146.

64. ———. "The Effect of Rearing Conditions on Behavior." In *Sex Research: New Developments,* ed. J. Money, pp. 161–175. New York: Holt, Rinehart & Winston, 1965.

65. HARTMANN, H. (1939). *Ego Psychology and the Problem of Adaptation.* New York: International Universities Press, 1958.

66. HEATH, R. G. "Pleasure and Brain Activity in Man." *J. Nerv. Ment. Dis.* 154 (1972): 3–18.

67. HOLBROOK, D. *Sex and Dehumanization.* London: Pitman, 1972.

68. HOOKER, E. "The Adjustment of the Male Overt Homosexual." *J. Proj. Tech.* 21 (1957): 18–31.

69. IVERSON, W. *Venus U.S.A.* New York: Pocket Books, 1970.

70. JOHNSON, A. M., and SZUREK, S. A. "The Genesis of Antisocial Acting Out in Children and Adults." *Psychoanal. Q.* 21 (1952): 323–343.

226

PERVERSION

71. JOST, A. "A New Look at the Mechanisms Controlling Sex Differentiation in Mammals." *Johns Hopkins Med. J.* 130 (1972): 38–53.

72. KALLMANN, F. J. "A Comparative Twin Study on the Genetic Aspects of Male Homosexuality." *J. Nerv. Ment. Dis.* 115 (1952): 283–298.

73. KARLEN, A. *Sexuality and Homosexuality.* New York: W. W. Norton & Co., 1971.

74. KHAN, M. M. R. "Clinical Aspects of the Schizoid Technique." *Int. J. Psycho-Anal.* 41 (1960): 430–437.

75. ———. "Foreskin Fetishism and Its Relation to Ego Pathology in a Male Homosexual." *Int. J. Psycho-Anal.* 46 (1965): 64–80.

76. ———. "The Function of Intimacy and Acting Out in the Perversions." In *Sexual Behavior and the Law,* ed. R. Slovenko, pp. 397–412. Springfield, Ill.: Charles C Thomas, 1965.

77. KINSEY, A. C.; POMEROY, W. B.; and MARTIN, C. E. *Sexual Behavior in the Human Male.* Philadelphia: W. B. Saunders Co., 1948.

78. ———, et al. *Sexual Behavior in the Human Female.* Philadelphia: W. B. Saunders Co., 1953.

79. KLAF, F. S. "Female Sexuality and Paranoid Schizophrenia." *Arch. Gen Psychiat.* 1 (1961): 84–86.

80. KLEEMAN, J. A. "The Establishment of Core Gender Identity in Normal Girls." *Arch. Sex. Behav.* 1 (1971): 103–129.

81. KLEIN, H. R., and HORWITZ, W. A. "Psycho-sexual Factors in the Paranoid Phenomena." *Am. J. Psychiat.* 105 (1949): 697–701.

82. KLEIN, M. *The Psychoanalysis of Children.* London: Hogarth Press, 1932.

83. KOLODNY, R. C.; MASTERS, W. H.; HENDRYX, J.; et al. "Plasma Testosterone and Serum Analysis in Male Homosexuals." *N. Engl. J. Med.* 285 (1971): 1170–1174.

84. KREUZ, L. E.; ROSE, R. M.; and JENNINGS, J. R. "Suppression of Plasma Testosterone Levels and Psychological Stress." *Arch. Gen. Psychiat.* 26 (1972): 479–482.

85. LASCHET, U. "Antiandrogen in the Treatment of Sex

Offenders: Mode of Action and Therapeutic Outcome." In *Contemporary Sexual Behavior: Critical Issues in the 1970s,* ed. J. Zubin and J. Money, pp. 311–319. Baltimore: Johns Hopkins Press, 1973.

86. LEITES, N. *The New Ego: Psychoanalytic Concepts.* New York: Science House, 1971.

87. LORENZ, K. *King Solomon's Ring.* New York: Thomas Y. Crowell Co., 1952.

88. MACALPINE, I., and HUNTER, R. A. *David Paul Schreber: Memoirs of My Mental Illness.* London: Dawson & Sons, 1955.

89. MACLEAN, P. D. "Studies on the Cerebral Representation of Certain Basic Sexual Functions." In *Brain and Behavior,* vol. 3, ed. R. A. Gorski and R. E. Whalen, pp. 35–79. Los Angeles: University of California Press, 1966.

90. MAHLER, M. S. "On Child Psychosis and Schizophrenia: Autistic and Symbiotic Infantile Psychoses." *Psychoanal. Study Child* 7 (1952): 286–305. New York: International Universities Press.

91. ———. "Autism and Symbiosis, Two Extreme Disturbances of Identity." *Int. J. Psycho-Anal.* 39 (1958): 77–83.

92. ———. "Thoughts About Development and Individuation." *Psychoanal. Study Child* 18 (1963): 307–324. New York: International Universities Press.

93. ———. "On the Significance of the Normal Separation-Individuation Phase: With Reference to Research in Symbiotic Child Psychosis." In *Drives, Affects, Behavior,* vol. 2, ed. M. Schur. New York: International Universities Press, 1965.

94. ———. *On Human Symbiosis and the Vicissitudes of Individuation,* vol. 1. New York: International Universities Press, 1968.

95. ———. "Rapprochement Subphase of the Separation-Individuation Process." *Psychoanal. Q.* 41 (1972): 487–506.

96. ———, and FURER, M. "Certain Aspects of the Separation-Individuation Phase." *Psychoanal. Q.* 32 (1963): 1–14.

97. MALINOWSKI, B. *Sex and Repression in Savage Society.* New York: Humanities Press, 1927.

98. MARGOLESE, M. S. "Homosexuality: A New Endocrine Correlate." *Hormones and Behavior* 1 (1970): 151–155.

99. MARMOR, J. "Orality in the Hysterical Personality." *J. Am. Psychoanal. Assoc.* 1 (1953): 656–671.

100. ———. " 'Normal' and 'Deviant' Sexual Behavior." *J.A.M.A.* 217 (1971): 165–170.

101. ———. ed. *Sexual Inversion.* New York: Basic Books, 1965.

102. MASTERS, W. H., and JOHNSON, V. E. *Human Sexual Response.* Boston: Little, Brown & Co., 1966.

103. MCDOUGALL, J. "Primal Scene and Sexual Perversion." *Int. J. Psycho-Anal.* 53 (1972): 371–384.

104. MICHAEL, R. P. "Biological Factors in the Organization and Expression of Sexual Behavior." In *The Pathology and Treatment of Sexual Deviation,* ed. I. Rosen, pp. 24–54. New York: Oxford University Press, 1964.

105. MILLER, I. "Unconscious Fantasy and Masturbatory Technique." *J. Am. Psychoanal. Assoc.* 17 (1969): 826–847.

106. MILLETT, K. *Sexual Politics.* New York: Doubleday & Co., 1970.

107. MODLIN, H. C. "Psychodynamics and Management of Paranoid States in Women." *Arch. Gen. Psychiat.* 8 (1963): 263–268.

108. MONEY, J. "Sex Reassignment as Related to Hermaphroditism and Transsexualism." In *Transsexualism and Sex Reassignment,* ed. R. Green and J. Money, pp. 91–115. Baltimore: Johns Hopkins Press, 1969.

109. ———, and EHRHARDT, A. *Man and Woman, Boy and Girl.* Baltimore: Johns Hopkins Press, 1972.

110. ———, and POLLITT, E. "Psychogenetic and Psychosexual Ambiguities: Klinefelter's Syndrome and Transvestism Compared." *Arch. Gen. Psychiat.* 11 (1964): 589–595.

111. MOORE, B. "Frigidity: A Review of the Psychoanalytic Literature." *Psychoanal. Q.* 33 (1964): 323–349.

112. NEWMAN, L. E., and STOLLER, R. J. "The Oedipal Situa-

tion in Male Transsexualism." *Br. J. Med. Psychol.* 44 (1971): 295–303.

113. OLDS, J. "Self-stimulation Experiments and Differential Reward Systems." In *Reticular Formation of the Brain,* ed. H. H. Jasper, L. D. Proctor, R. S. Knighton, W. C. Noshay, and R. T. Costello, pp. 671–687. Boston: Little, Brown & Co., 1958.

114. OSTOW, M., ed. *Sexual Deviation: Psychoanalytic Insights.* New York: Quadrangle Books, 1974.

115. PARE, C. M. B. "Etiology of Homosexuality: Genetic and Chromosomal Aspects." In *Sexual Inversion,* ed. J. Marmor, pp. 70–80. New York: Basic Books, 1965.

116. PFEIFFER, E., ed. *Sigmund Freud and Lou Andreas-Salomé: Letters.* New York: Harcourt Brace Jovanovich, 1972.

117. PILLARD, R. C.; ROSE, R. M.; and SHERWOOD, M. "Plasma Testosterone Levels in Homosexual Men." *Arch. Sex. Behav.* 3 (1974): 453–457.

118. RACHMAN, S. "Sexual Fetishism: An Experimental Analogue." *Psychol. Record* 16 (1966): 293–296.

119. RACKER, H. *Transference and Countertransference.* New York: International Universities Press, 1968.

120. REICH, W. "The Phallic-Narcissistic Character." In *Character Analysis,* pp. 200–207. New York: Orgone Institute Press, 1949.

121. *The Report of the Commission on Obscenity and Pornography.* New York: Bantam Books, 1970.

122. ROEDER, R. C. "Homosexuality 'Burned Out': German Surgeon Claims Hypothalamotomy Normalizes Sex Drive." *Medical World News,* September 25, 1970, pp. 20–21.

123. ROSENFELD, H. "Remarks on the Relation of Male Homosexuality to Paranoia, Paranoid Anxiety and Narcissism." *Int. J. Psycho-Anal.* 30 (1949): 36–47.

124. SCHMIDEBERG, M. "Deliquent Acts as Perversions and Fetiches." *Br. J. Delinq.* 7 (1956): 44–49.

125. SEARLES, H. F. "Sexual Processes in Schizophrenia." *Psychiatry* 24 (1961): 87–95.

126. SEARS, R. R.; MACCOBY, E. E.; and LEVIN, H. *Patterns of Child Rearing.* Evanston, Ill.: Row, Peterson & Co., 1957.

127. SHERFEY, M. J. "The Evolution and Nature of Female Sexuality in Relation to Psychoanalytic Theory." *J. Am. Psychoanal. Assoc.* 14 (1966): 28–128.

128. SLATER, E. "Birth Order and Maternal Age of Homosexuals." *Lancet* 1–1 (1962): 69–71.

129. SMIRNOFF, V. N. "The Masochistic Contract." *Int. J. Psycho-Anal.* 50 (1969): 665–671.

130. SOCARIDES, C. W. *The Overt Homosexual.* New York: Grune & Stratton, 1968.

131. ――――. "Homosexuality and Medicine." *JAMA* 212 (1970): 1199–1202.

132. ――――. "The Demonified Mother: A Study of Voyeurism and Sexual Sadism." *Int. Rev. Psycho-Anal.* 1 (1974): 187–195.

133. SPITZ, R. A. *The First Year of Life.* New York: International Universities Press, 1965.

134. STOLLER, R. J. "The Hermaphroditic Identity of Hermaphrodites." *J. Nerv. Ment. Dis.* 139 (1964): 453–457.

135. ――――. "The Mother's Contribution to Infantile Transvestic Behavior." *Int. J. Psycho-Anal.* 47 (1966): 384–395.

136. ――――. "Shakespearean Tragedy: Coriolanus." *Psychoanal. Q.* 35 (1966): 263–274.

137. ――――. *Sex and Gender,* vol. 1. New York: Science House, 1968.

138. ――――. "The Transsexual Boy: Mother's Feminized Phallus." *Br. J. Med. Psychol.* 43 (1970): 117–128.

139. ――――. "The Term 'Transvestism.' " *Arch. Gen. Psychiat.* 24 (1971): 230–237.

140. ――――. "The 'Bedrock' of Masculinity and Femininity: Bisexuality." *Arch. Gen. Psychiat.* 26 (1972): 207–212.

141. ――――. "Etiological Factors in Female Transsexualism: A First Approximation." *Arch. Sex. Behav.* 2 (1972): 47–64.

142. ――――. "Transsexualism and Transvestism." *Psychiatric Annals* 1 (1972): 6–72.

143. ――――. "The Impact of New Advances in Sex Research on Psychoanalytic Theory." *Am. J. Psychiat.* 130 (1973): 241–251, 1207–1216.

144. ――――. "The Male Transsexual as 'Experiment.' " *Int. J. Psycho-Anal.* 54 (1973): 215–226.

145. ———. "Psychoanalysis and Physical Intervention in the Brain." In *Contemporary Sexual Behavior: Critical Issues in the 1970s*, ed. J. Zubin and J. Money, pp. 339–350. Baltimore: Johns Hopkins Press, 1973.

146. ———. *Splitting: A Case of Female Masculinity.* New York: Quadrangle Books, 1973.

147. ———. *Sex and Gender,* vol. 2. New York: Jason Aronson, 1975.

148. ———, and NEWMAN, L. E. "The Bisexual Identity of Transsexuals: Two Case Examples." *Arch. Sex. Behav.* 1 (1971): 17–28.

149. TOURNEY, G., and HATFIELD, L. "Androgen Metabolism in Schizophrenics, Homosexuals, and Normal Controls." *Biol. Psychiat.* 6 (1973): 23–36.

150. VANGGAARD, T. *Phallós: A Symbol and Its History in the Male World.* New York: International Universities Press, 1972.

151. WALINDER, J. *Transsexualism: A Study of Forty-three Cases.* Göteborg: Scandinavian University Books, 1967.

152. WERMER, H., and LEVING, S. "Masturbation Fantasies." *Psychoanal. Study Child* 22 (1967): 315–328. New York: International Universities Press.

153. WHITE, R. B. "The Mother-Conflict in Schreber's Psychosis." *Int. J. Psycho-Anal.* 42 (1961): 55–73.

154. WILLIAMS, A. H. "The Psychopathology and Treatment of Sexual Murderers." In *The Pathology and Treatment of Sexual Deviation: A Methodological Approach,* ed. I. Rosen, pp. 351–377. New York: Oxford University Press, 1964.

155. WINNICOTT, D. W. (1960). "Ego Distortion in Terms of True or False Self." In *The Maturational Processes and the Facilitating Environment: Studies in the Theory of Emotional Development.* New York: International Universities Press, 1972.

Index

aberrant sexual behavior, ix–x, 34–41. *See also* perversions; variants
  in animals, 36, 37–8, 52–3
  behavioral theories, 40–1
  biological factors, 92–3
  defined, 3, 6
  fixations in, 34–5
  physical explanations, 37–9
  research in, xiii–xiv
  self-created, 36
  statistical explanation, 37, 41–2
adolescence. *See* childhood
aggression, 21, 44–5, 106 *n.*, 112–13
  and maleness, 149, 150
  toward parents, 121 *n.*–122 *n.*
anal phase, 15 *n.*, 32
androgen, in prenatal development, 16, 17, 46–7
androgen insensitivity syndrome, 16, 47
animal behavior, xv, 36–8, 40–1, 56
  vs. human behavior, 20–2, 52–3
  prenatal development, 16, 46–7
anthropology, 45. *See also* cultural relativism
anxiety, xiv, xvii–xviii, 7–8, 105, 106 *n.*, 118. *See also* trauma and triumph
  childhood, 98–100, 159
  and pornography, 86–7

symbiosis, 135–62, 148, 149–52, 154–6

Bak, R. C., 132
behaviorism. *See* conditioning
bestiality, 51
Bieber, Irving, 199
binding perversions, 56, 58, 67–8
biopsychic mechanisms, 146–7
birth control, 217
bisexuality, 14, 15 and *n.*, 16–19, 144
  Freud's theory of, 18–19, 144
  inherited tendencies, 35
  in prenatal development, 16–17
Blumer, D., 38, 47
Boehm, R., 157–8
boredom, 7, 9, 107–8, 114, 115–16
  familiarity in, 116 and *n.*
  and sexual excitement, 70 *n.*
Boss, M., 106 *n.*
brain abnormalities, 4, 38, 47–8, 198
brain studies, 21–2, 44
  hypersexuality, 37–8
  midbrain mechanisms, 39
  pleasure centers, 33
  temporal lobe epilepsy, 38, 47–8
breasts, 4, 157–8, 176, 181, 185–6